Praise for *Sales Coaching*

The single most important sales management skill is coaching! Linda has written the best book on sales coaching that we have ever seen! Make the leap from sales manager to sales coach and watch your performance skyrocket! Put this book on your must read list!

Mike and Joe
Cofounders, The SalesRoundup Podcast

Outstanding! Linda has succeeded in distilling years of effective sales coaching experience into a 5-step coaching model. This concise and first-rate guide should be on every sales manager's short list of required reading.

Jeff Blackwell
Founder, SalesPractice.com

The best sales managers are sales coaches first. Linda's simple and practical approach is the best I have seen to turn bosses into coaches and salespeople into sales champions. Use this and I promise you that everybody around you will be better and your numbers will be stronger.

Marc Bassin
Executive Coach

As the world restructures the way that firms operate toward boundaryless management systems, the role of managers as mentors and coaches becomes imperative. Richardson has developed very powerful and practical coaching techniques for management as well as selling.

Ian MacMillan
Executive Director, The Wharton School
University of Pennsylvania

Linda Richardson's techniques are simple, practical, and effective. Even the most seasoned sales managers will find this book an excellent refresher, while newer sales managers will experience *instant* improvement in their coaching effectiveness.

Christine Troianello
Performance Improvement Manager
Lucent Technologies

This is a first-class, quick-reading, practical book for all sales managers.

Ron Galotti
Publisher, Vogue

I have just read *Sales Coaching* for the first time. I say first time because I will read it many more times, as I want to grasp the skills and spiritual part of coaching to practice coaching at the highest level, which is self-coaching. I do not say sales coaching because this book is superb for all types of coaching.

Shigeru Sato
Consultant, Corporate Marketing and Public Relations
Sumitomo 3M Limited

Sales organizations can be sure of two things—more complex sales situations and more competition. When we recruit for salespeople we are adamant about hiring people that can constantly adjust. This is the essence of the message in Linda's book. Salespeople must be open to coaching, but their sales managers must encourage self-analysis, and invest the time to coach. Linda is the ultimate coach in moving from being a "boss to coach" to build a sales team that wins.

Lou Eccleston
Executive Managing Director
Standard & Poor's

A major league hit. Linda takes the mystery of coaching and turns it into magic for management.

Josh Hammon
Author of The Stuff Americans Are Made Of

With the evolution of the sales process from product to solution and from presentation to consultation, Linda's work is a must read. If you do not embrace Linda's methodology, you will be outsold by those who do!

David P. Choate
Senior Vice President
Capital Institutional Services, Inc.

Successful sales organizations make sales coaching a part of how they do business every day. Linda's book is the best I have read to turn managers into coaches with the goal of developing highly competitive winning, sales teams.

Wallace W. Gardner, Jr.
Worldwide Sales Manager
Chubb and Son, Inc.

Sales organizations realize the dramatic impact sales coaching has on improving performance. Linda's book is an excellent source for turning sales managers into sales coaches that produce results.

Jim Steele
Chief Customer Officer and President
Salesforce.com

Good coaching yields great performance. Linda's pioneering first edition took sales managers from boss to coach a decade ago. With this second edition, she takes sales coaches to sales champion levels.

Gerhard Gschwandtner
Founder and Publisher
Selling Power Magazine

Other Books by Linda Richardson

Perfect Selling

20 Lessons to Open and Close Sales Now

Selling by Phone

Stop Telling, Start Selling

SALES COACHING

MAKING THE GREAT LEAP FROM
SALES MANAGER TO SALES COACH

SECOND EDITION

Linda Richardson

New York | Chicago | San Francisco | Lisbon | London
Madrid | Mexico City | Milan | New Delhi
San Juan | Seoul | Singapore | Sydney | Toronto

1 2 3 4 5 6 7 8 9 0   FGR/FGR   0 1 0 9 8

ISBN: 978-0-07-160380-5
MHID: 0-07-160380-8

This publication is designed to provide accurate and authoritative information in regard to the subject matter covered. It is sold with the understanding that the publisher is not engaged in rendering legal, accounting, or other professional service. If legal advice or other expert assistance is required, the services of a competent professional person should be sought.

> —*From a declaration of principles jointly adopted by a committee of the American Bar Association and a committee of publishers.*

McGraw-Hill books are available at special quantity discounts to use as premiums and sales promotions, or for use in corporate training programs. To contact a representative please visit the Contact Us pages at www.mhprofessional.com.

To my parents,
Connie and Alfred,
who guided my life
and
will live forever in my heart

Contents

Why This Second Edition?

A decade has passed. There have been two major changes in sales coaching that warrant a second edition: (1) the increase in awareness in sales organizations about the critical need for sales coaching to improve performance, achieve revenue growth, and retain their salespeople, and (2) the advances in technology and tools that are now available to sales managers to help them plan sales strategies and prioritize and direct their coaching efforts. As I worked on the book, I also found opportunity after opportunity to refine and build on almost all of the content to such an extent that this is all but a new book.

My goal in 1996 when I wrote the book was not only to provide a how-to sales coaching guide for sales managers, but also to raise awareness that sales coaching was the most important strategy an organization could employ to raise the productivity and morale of its sales force. In 1996, many organizations were paying little more than lip service to the importance of sales coaching. Sales coaching wasn't recognized or rewarded.

Today, companies are seeking out ways to achieve revenue growth, and most recognize that sales is an area they can dramatically improve by focusing on it. As a result, they now view sales coaching as the primary strategy to make salespeople more productive and achieve revenue growth.

As I worked through my book, it was clear how much had changed. Today, while most sales organizations can't claim that they have a sales coaching discipline in place, they are actively moving in that direction by applying resources to turn their sales managers into sales coaches.

But making sales coaching a part of the fiber of sales management remains a struggle for most organizations. The good news today is that there is awareness and there are new tools. Executives, sales managers, and salespeople alike realize that sales coaching is the link between sales strategy and successful execution of the strategy. Technology can provide sales managers with data that free up their time from mundane management issues to allow them to be more strategic. Technology is giving them the information and metrics they need to follow opportunities through all stages of the sales cycle to provide the resources and support needed. It also gives them hard data to complement their observations and perceptions and help them target their coaching efforts.

The revisions to this book are significant. Changes include streamlining of the Developmental Sales Coaching Model, addressing remote coaching, and discussing technology and tools. While the underlying process of sales coaching presented in the 1996 book remains true, the level of awareness has changed, organizations have changed, markets and competitors have changed, technology has changed, sales forces have changed, and I have changed, and so this feels like a new book.

The great news is that in the decade that has passed, most sales organizations are ready, willing, and struggling to make sales coaching a part of their DNA. The 10 years since the first edition have added to my experience of working with clients to build sales cultures and transform sales managers into sales coaches.

Today, the job of the sales coach is more challenging than ever. It is also more important then ever. The environment is ripe. Salespeople need coaching. It is a privilege to be your sales coach in this second edition.

Introduction

Sales coaching is for everybody, every day. It is the most critical competitive skill that any sales organization can have. It is the most potent tool available for improving sales performance, maximizing productivity, and achieving revenue growth. The goal of sales coaching is to increase performance by helping sales managers make the most of their organization's resources—starting with their salespeople.

The first objective of this book is to help you make the leap from manager to coach, so that sales coaching becomes an integral part of how you manage. The broader objective is to help you create a sales culture first with your team and then with your organization.

This book tells why sales coaching is the most critical part of your job as a sales manager and why it is the best vehicle you have for helping your team achieve and exceed goals. As you increase your effectiveness as a *sales coach*, you will transform your salespeople, helping them make the journey from ordinary to extraordinary. You will see them take responsibility for their own development. You will build a cohesive sales team that not only performs but can *coach itself*. Sales coaching will help you accelerate the sales productivity of your salespeople and strengthen your relationships with them.

Leadership is about vision. It is about making the future better. The first step in leadership is vision. The second step is empowerment. The third step is coaching. While all three are interrelated, the only one that pervades all three is coaching—that is how you get better at the other two.

As a sales manager, your sales leadership is what makes each day better for your sales team. There are two ways to get better: work harder and/or change.

Your sales coaching will help your salespeople see other possibilities and do things differently. You and your salespeople are your organization's most valuable assets. If you are not improving every day, your organization cannot benefit from your talents or remain competitive. Every organization and every sales professional has blind spots. Sales coaching turns those blind spots into perspective.

Sales coaching starts with you. You have two tasks: to coach your direct reports and to get coaching for yourself. Even if your organization has a compelling vision and is technically advanced, without developmental sales coaching as a way of life and feedback as a mainstay of communication, your management and your sales force cannot *continuously* improve and get to the next level *fast* enough. Organizations that knit sales coaching into their DNA will be the winners.

The purpose of this book is to help ensure that you have the heart, knowledge, skills, and tools you need to make sales coaching a part of how you lead your team. The sales coaching approach in this book is not about long, laborious coaching sessions. It's about taking short spurts of time to help salespeople improve, become responsible for their own development, and create an environment of support in which this happens. It is a strategy for helping all the members of your sales team meet their objectives.

The benefits of sales coaching are many. Performance improvement certainly is at the top of the list, but sales coaching is also the key to retention and stronger relationships. Becoming a sales coach even makes "the boss"—the evaluator—part of your role a lot easier because coaching helps eliminate disappointing surprises and leads to much better evaluations.

The Developmental Sales Coaching Model covered in this book is powerful. If all it did was help salespeople become more productive and successful, that would be enough. But it also teaches salespeople how to self-coach and remove their own obstacles, and it fosters peer coaching and self-coaching so that salespeople learn how to find their own answers and the learning is continuous and consistent.

The model is *developmental*, which means that you work on one priority at a time. Not only does this achieve the best and fastest results, but it is time efficient in that you can coach in 15 minutes or less. Initially, when you are coaching your salespeople, their dependency on you as the coach is higher. But the more you coach, the less their dependence.

Sales management without sales coaching is equivalent to management of a sports team without a coach. It's unheard of. Your salespeople will "play" better and win more with you as their coach.

Most of the sales managers we work with want to coach. Most of the salespeople we work with tell us that they are hungry for coaching and feedback. Yet many salespeople say that they don't get feedback on how they are doing—unless it is to tell them that they are doing something wrong. They complain that their sales managers don't take the initiative to coach them. Sales managers say that salespeople don't ask for coaching from them. Everyone is acutely aware of the need for continuous improvement to remain competitive. Many sales managers see sales coaching as the path to continuous improvement, but they aren't sure how to coach. One sales manager expressed what many feel when he said, "I'm wondering if what I do when I 'coach' is really coaching."

Being the sales coach to six, eight, or more salespeople can seem as if it takes Spartan strength. You may not have many role models to follow. The culture of your organization may not be there yet. There may even be a bias against coaching.

You can take the leap from manager to coach. You can transform your team, yourself, and even your organization. You as the sales coach can use each day to increase the performance of your team and get better and stronger and win again and again.

*S*tructure says boss.

*R*elationship says coach.

1

Developmental Sales Coaching—Boss to Coach

Organizations today must adjust to change with more speed and insight than ever before. As a sales manager, you are on the front line of that change. You are close to external and internal customers. You make the inside-outside connection. You are in the field near customers. You are on the inside track. You are the link between executive management and the sales force. Your sales coaching is the lifeline for your sales team.

Sales coaching is a process, but more than that, it is a way of life. It is visceral—a gut-level feeling that helps determine how you work with your salespeople and how your managers work with you. It is a commitment among professionals to support one another so that they can be the best they can be.

How much sales coaching do you provide? Richardson research with more than 1,000 managers and 4,500 salespeople showed that many sales managers are simply not coaching to the level that they could be or that is needed. In our study, sales managers were rated as coaches on a scale of 1.0 to 5.0. Managers who scored a 4.5 out of

5.0 were classified as world-class sales coaches. The average score for all sales managers participating in the research, however, was 3.5 out of the possible 5.0, and the higher scores among the behaviors were in the areas of rapport, encouragement, and "telling" salespeople what to do rather than collaborating in developing problem solving skills. But scores fell off most in the areas of preparation, involving salespeople in the problem solving, providing clear feedback with examples, agreeing to specific measurable action plans, and follow-up. The subset items in the study showed that most managers fall squarely into a "Let me tell you" expert coaching model rather than an interactive approach in which salespeople analyze and remove their own obstacles.

Salespeople rated their sales managers about 13 percent lower than the sales managers rated themselves. This may be attributed to sales managers' tendency to seeing themselves through their intentions and direct reports basing their responses on their perceptions of what they experience.

How do you work with your salespeople? Boss or coach? We asked hundreds of sales managers for their ideas about what it takes to be an effective sales coach. Specifically, we have asked them what words come to mind when they think of "coach." They use words like *role model, collaborate, add value, communicate, guide,* and *support.* Many describe a coach, teacher, or parent who may have pushed them hard but who believed in them and helped them succeed.

Compare that to the synonyms they used to describe "boss": *control, authority, title, power, position, status,* and *dictate.* Webster defines *boss* as a person "in authority over employees," and the verb *boss* means "to order about," as in "Do this. Do that." Think about the best manager you ever had. Did the relationship feel like peer to peer or boss to subordinate?

How do you want to work with your salespeople? The more you coach, the less you'll have to boss. How much of a priority is sales coaching for you—10 percent, 20 percent, . . . 80 percent of your time? One sales manager rated himself a great coach. Why? He said, "My door is always open. My people know that they can come to me when they need me." Certainly this sales manager might be a

> *The more you coach, the less you'll have to boss.*

very effective coach when the opportunity *presents itself*, but reactive coaching is just one part of coaching.

Zones

How ready are you and your team for sales coaching? It is important for the sales coach and the salespeople to be in the right "cultural space" for sales coaching. The word for cultural space is *zone*.

When you think about your job, or the job of your salespeople, you probably think in terms of your role, title, skills, and competencies. Although these things define *what* you do, it's important that you step back and look at *how* you and your salespeople approach your jobs—and your lives. One way to take a step back is to understand the *culture zones* that you, your team, and your organization are living in.

There are five zones: the Dead Zone, the Comfort Zone, the Panic Zone, the Depression Zone, and the Stretch Zone. Everyone lives and works—usually in that order—predominantly in *one* zone. Certainly there is movement back and forth, but most people stabilize in one place—at least for a period of time.

In which zone do you think the best learning takes place? Which zone is conducive to change?

Some sales managers and salespeople believe that they learn and produce best in the Panic Zone. They believe this is where they are most productive. But when they are asked to look at what they mean by "panic," they usually talk about the exhilaration and excitement connected with the energy that they feel. This is quite different from the fear generated in the Panic Zone.

Other sales managers believe that they and salespeople produce best in the Comfort Zone because that is where they don't feel threatened and so can be more effective and productive. While this seems reasonable, comfort can easily get stagnant. We all know companies that once were global leaders that stabilized in the Comfort Zone, only to watch their competitive edge disappear.

Let's look at each of these five zones to help you consider where you and your team are now and where you want to be.

The Dead Zone

People who live in this zone are not actively interested in improving. They take no initiative to improve. *They stay the same*, and they don't seek ways to change. Typically they feel that *things happen to them*. They are resigned to things *as they are*, and, more important, *as they were*. They seek confirmation for their past in the present. They lack interest in the future. For whatever reason, they are disengaged. In today's competitive environment, no sales organizations can tolerate team members who are in this zone.

The Comfort Zone

By contrast, professionals who are in the Comfort Zone *want* to be effective. They've been successful in the past, and they want to continue to be successful. Their strategy, which on the surface looks reasonable, is to repeat what worked for them in the past. The Comfort Zone is very seductive for that very reason. It is natural for people to reproduce what made them successful in the past. Unfortunately, this is a dangerous strategy because the world around them is changing fast. Everything in their world is changing—everything but them. People in this zone are willing to *fine-tune* in response to change but don't see a need for proactive change.

They think of themselves as open. They are smart, and they work hard. Usually there is little feedback, curiosity, expectations, or sales coaching to help them *break out of the Comfort Zone.*

The Panic Zone

Too many sales organizations spend too much time here. This is the zone of reactive adjustment. What's good about the Panic Zone is that it grabs attention. Professionals who are in the Panic Zone care very much, or they wouldn't panic. The problem is that panic is debilitating. People who feel panicked can't learn or perform well. Their judgment is impaired. They don't make good decisions. Their quality suffers. And burnout in a few months or even a few weeks— not years—is common. People who are in this zone feel indecisive and unable to handle what needs to be done. Turnover is high. In extreme cases, people can feel paralyzed.

Life is not fun in the Panic Zone. In the long run, panic doesn't give energy. It takes it. It *creates exhaustion—diminishing and draining talented professionals.* Think about the Olympic skater who could do a triple-axel jump yesterday but not today.

Professionals who are in the Panic Zone know that the old systems aren't working, but they are often at a loss as to what to do about that. They often blame their organizations, not themselves. They do not feel in control. *Winding up in the Panic Zone is often caused by staying in the Comfort Zone too long.*

The Depression Zone

This zone is the result of sustained participation in a miserable situation. Organizations, teams, or individuals who stay in the Panic Zone too long can often move into the Depression Zone. One client described this zone as the War Zone, and articles in the press over the next month justified the description.

The Stretch Zone

The Stretch Zone is paradise compared to any of the other zones. It is a good place to live and work. Professionals who are in the Stretch Zone are actively involved in their work and are committed to developing themselves. They look for ways to change. They *intentionally* do things differently so that they can at least stay in sync with change. They are not threatened, for example, by technology and new ways of doing things. The Stretch Zone is the best environment for coaching because salespeople are willing to seek out feedback or at least are open to feedback to learn how they can improve. Of course, it is important to respect and protect what is good and positive, and also at the same time to actively seek ways to improve. Sales managers and salespeople who are in the Stretch Zone believe that their actions control what happens to them.

There is only one problem with the Stretch Zone: it is hard to be there all the time and almost impossible to be there all alone. *That's where coaching by you is essential.* The way you work with your salespeople determines how willing they are to join you in the Stretch Zone. They must trust you and believe that you are there to help them succeed and add value, not just to evaluate them or catch them doing something wrong. It takes confidence for salespeople to step out and stretch, try new things, and expose their vulnerabilities and not just their strengths to you—for example, to tell you about the big deal they think they may lose rather than hiding it from you until it is too late for you to coach and add resources to it.

Sales coaching makes the dynamic of stretching possible. The deal between you and your salespeople is that you will help them and they will help each other overcome their obstacles. The space needed for the Stretch Zone is that of support, not fear. If you think about a coach who made a difference in your life, perhaps an athletic coach or a teacher, you know what it feels like to have support and have someone in your corner. You don't have to be best friends with your salespeople, but you must care about them and let them know you are committed to their success.

Stretch is a model of potential, because no one ever gets to the outer perimeter. Sales coaching is your tool to help your salespeople stretch and continue to change and improve. There is *always* room to get better. There is very little change or growth without coaching and support.

The way you work with your salespeople determines how willing they are to join you in the Stretch Zone.

It takes you as a coach, not a boss, to help your salespeople and your team move into and sustain the Stretch Zone. To understand the difference between the structure of a relationship and the dynamics of a relationship, think about a direct report with whom you have a great working relationship. How do you work with her—as a boss or as a peer? The answer is probably as a peer. The reporting structure may be that of boss-subordinate, but the dynamics of the relationship is that of peer-team. The boss-subordinate structure doesn't have to generate boss-subordinate relationships. There are times to boss, such as performance evaluation, but not when you are trying to coach. Even in the most hierarchical environment, the good news is that creating a coaching "spirit" of support is possible. You, as one sales manager, can change the dynamic of how you work with your people.

Salespeople, particularly those new to the workforce, are demanding sales coaching. One sales manager discussed how today's salespeople have changed and how they expect support. "We all need to learn about coaching—how to give it and how to receive it. If we can accomplish this in our organization, we can differentiate ourselves from our competition and succeed."

You, as well as your organization, determine what zone you are in. So in thinking about zones, check *your* own zone, not just the zone of your organization. The open questions for your life and your work are: In which zone do you want to be? In which zone do you want your sales team to be? What will you do to help your people and you get and stay in that zone?

Boss versus Coach

The goal of sales coaching is much like the goal of parenting—to create independence. There are times when it is necessary to call the shots, but there are many more times when you should elicit input from your salespeople and encourage them to come up with the answers and take

responsibility. Frank, a new senior manager, inherited a team of salespeople who, while they were high performers, had been schooled under the previous manager to act in a totally dependent way. The solution to any challenge that was even

> *You, as well as your organization, determine what zone you are in.*

slightly important was, "Ask Frank!" For example, they checked *all* pricing with him *all* the time. Through coaching, he *empowered* his salespeople to handle most of the pricing situations that had previously found their way to his door. Working within strategic pricing guidelines set by management, he coached his team to confidently and effectively preserve price and maintain relationships.

He implemented coaching plans with each of his salespeople to reinforce and build on their skills. His coaching helped his salespeople change their attitudes and work with their customers more effectively. He fostered their negotiating deals independently. They were successful—100 percent of his team met goal. His relationships with his team members were strengthened. His team became the role model corporatewide for executing a new pricing policy that was vital to the company's profitability.

Sunday's game may be the time to shout and set up plays, but what happens the other six days will determine how well the plays are executed during the game. The idea that "real" sales managers "boss" is all but gone.

The "soft" side of Developmental Sales Coaching is soft where it should be soft—on salespeople. The hard side is hard where it should be hard—on accountability and measurement. There is a time to develop and a time to evaluate. And not simultaneously. Today, soft is hard. Soft skills are to hard skills what software is to hardware.

The goal of sales coaching is much like the goal of parenting— to create independence.

When salespeople are involved, they generate their own motivation. They, not external forces such as the carrot (reward) or the stick (punishment), are the motivators. When salespeople have input, they are much more inclined to buy in and be turned on and change. Rather than the carrot or the stick being the generator, internal drive becomes the generator. You want a motivated sales force. Motivational pep talks are fine because they help salespeople use what they have, but pep talks don't help them develop what they don't have. Certainly bonuses and prizes work, but these things are external forces that need constant replenishing, and the ante continues to increase (more carrots or bigger sticks are needed).

When salespeople don't feel that their voices are heard, when they experience "coaching" as evaluation and criticism, they lose heart and even the most motivated of them will gradually close down.

Most salespeople want to do a good job. They want to meet goal. They want to succeed. The Developmental Sales Coaching Model helps you coach them in a way that gives them a voice, a sense of control, and helps move them to the next level. It's in this kind of environment that salespeople and you can stretch and win.

Today it's not enough to avoid the valleys. You need a sales team that can reach the peaks. Consistent coaching will help you get to and sustain higher ground. You will take the valleys and flip them to peaks, and maintain the peaks to create higher ones.

Your mode of working with your people when you coach is up to you. Which do you think will bring about the best results—

boss or coach? With effective coaching, you'll have to boss less frequently.

Language says a lot about how an organization feels about sales coaching. Expressions like "sink or swim," "shape up or ship out," and "survival of the fittest" challenge the notion of coaching.

Even today, it is hard to find even one common business expression that reinforces sales coaching or even talks about sales coaching. One organization, a global leader in technology, that is a true model of the successful transition from boss to coach uses the expressions "Grow Yourself" and "Grow Your Team" as the mantra for its sales managers.

Certainly if an organization places a high priority on sales coaching, it's easier to make sales coaching a way of life. Fortunately, however, even without organizational support, *all* it takes is *your decision to take the initiative to coach*. You don't have to wait for approval from above. You can start coaching immediately by changing the *dynamics* of how you work with your salespeople, your managers, and your colleagues in other divisions.

You as a sales manager are in a unique position to be the catalyst to bring your sales team into the Stretch Zone to increase sales performance. You are in the right spot to see the adjustments that have to be made and to use sales coaching to make these adjustments. Your journey from boss to coach means placing the primary responsibility for learning not on training seminars but directly in your and your salespeople's hands and using coaching to help your salespeople become responsible for their own development.

Sales coaching builds on training and turns it into an *everyday* activity rather than an event. Today it is vital to shift the responsibility for development of salespeople from the "preachers" to the "practitioners." You and your salespeople must continuously assess your own strengths—coach to salesperson, salesperson to salesperson, and salesperson to coach. Of course, leverage formal training programs, e-learning, Webinars, podcasts, and other resources to jump-start the learning, develop expertise and skill, and create a common language, but it is you who keeps it going.

Sales coaching builds on training and turns it into an everyday activity rather than an event.

Begin by figuring out what factors are within your control and focus on them. Do you have the power to influence management, evaluation, compensation, and sales-force automation systems to support sales coaching? If so, good. If not, you can still have an impact. As you take measure, you will probably find far fewer limitations than you expected. Even in a worst-case scenario—a Dead Zone or Panic Zone culture—you can make a difference in your own sphere with your own salespeople by changing the zone. The deal is one that starts between you and one salesperson and expands from there to your team. The first step begins with your commitment to coach your salespeople to improve their sales performance and reach their goals. Moving from boss to coach is up to you.

A sales culture starts with you, your team, your division—or any two people who are ready to change how they work together.

Sales coaching is at the heart of a sales performance. Certainly creating a sales culture doesn't happen overnight. Convention holds that it takes three to five years to create a sales culture. However, this is not helpful considering the rate of change and the immediate needs of salespeople. The good news is that for your sales team, it takes only one thing: *you.* A sales culture starts with you, your team, your division—or any two people who are ready to change *how they work together. It can start now.*

*T*o win as a sales manager,

put sales coaching first.

2

Developmental Sales Coaching—Priority One

Your plate is full: setting objectives, establishing metrics, evaluating performance, market planning, managing the pipeline, generating reports, keeping up with and implementing new technology, recruiting—and the list goes on. While each of these is essential to your role, sales coaching is the key to releasing the power in everything else you do.

Sales coaching is *the secret* of sales success, of improving the performance of your sales team—and yourself. It is your most important job as a sales manager.

Study after study supports this. Bersen Associates in 2007, in one of the largest studies on corporate talent management, identified well-established coaching discipline as the number-one driver of impact among 22 top best practices. In a study of 2,000 salespeople by the Sales Executive Council, salespeople who received three or more hours of sales coaching per month on average reached 107 percent of their quota, as compared to 88 percent of quota for sales-people who received little or no coaching. In a study I participated in in conjunction with a Wharton School team to identify the characteristics of world-class sales organizations, one of the consistent factors we found across all of the 12 best-in-class sales organizations we studied was their commitment to and execution of sales coaching as their strategy to exceed goal and retain their salespeople. The top-performing sales managers differentiated themselves from all others through their emphasis on the sales coaching they provided to their direct reports. The Chally World-Class Sales Executive Report identified sales coaching as one of the top seven benchmarks of world-class sales organizations.

The data are compelling. It's not surprising, then, that sales organizations, which a decade ago gave not much more than lip service to sales coaching, have now made sales coaching a top priority and look to sales coaching to increase sales results dramatically. Management knows that without sales coaching, sales forces cannot change fast enough to keep up, remain competitive, and win. Effective sales coaching is the solution.

What Is Developmental Sales Coaching?

Developmental Sales Coaching is a *philosophy*, a discipline, and a process. It is a commitment to ongoing improvement. It is a methodology that will help you to help your salespeople identify and remove the obstacles—one at a time—that are in the way of their sales success. It is a safe forum where learning happens. It requires

> *Without sales coaching, sales forces cannot change fast enough to keep up, remain competitive, and win.*

commitment from both the salesperson and you. The skills of sales coaching are transferable from work to home.

Lots of things pass for sales coaching—everything from evaluation to a quick comment such as, "Good job." Developmental Sales Coaching is distinguished in three important ways:

- It uses a *coaching by asking* strategy to help salespeople learn how to analyze their own performance, take responsibility for their own development, find their own answers, and gain their buyer to the solution.

- It focuses on only *one priority* at a time to give issues the focus they require and accelerate change.

- It clearly *separates evaluation from development.* There is a place for both but not at the same time.

When these three things are in place, sales coaching is a powerful tool for achieving results and strengthening relationships.

As you use the Developmental Sales Coaching process, you guide your salespeople in analyzing their strengths and their areas for improvement. You learn where they are stuck and you help broaden their perspectives so they see other possibilities. You help them understand and remove their obstacles. You coach them through what otherwise would be a problem-solving maze to help them remove one obstacle and develop the skills to eventually remove many other obstacles themselves.

Sales Coaching Avoidance

Despite the emphasis placed on sales coaching by management today and the sincere desire on the part of the majority of sales managers to be effective sales coaches, few organizations yet have been able to make sales coaching a discipline of sales management.

When we ask sales managers what prevents them from sales coaching, they usually talk about a lack of time. In fact, their plates are full and time is a factor. However, my experience in over 25 years of working with thousands of sales managers and salespeople across all industries globally tells me that a lack of time isn't the real culprit. So what is blocking sales managers from making sales coaching a priority?

A number of factors:

- Many sales managers are not themselves coached, and lacking role models, don't coach.

- Many are not exactly sure how to coach. Without sales coaching training many simply lack the skills or the confidence to coach.

- Many are not incented or held accountable for coaching.

- Many are overwhelmed by administrative responsiblities.

- Many lack the tools to facilitate coaching.

- Many see sales coaching as confrontational and therefore something to avoid.

Among these obstacles, having no role models is the most serious. Lack of training is the easiest to fix. Sales managers quickly see that, far from being confrontational, sales coaching can be collaborative and supportive. In some organizations, headway is being made at holding sales managers accountable for sales coaching. For example, a number of sales organizations are tying sales coaching to reward and some are going so far as to require sales managers to record coaching sessions in their sales automation systems.

Sales coaching training is being provided and some organizations are so committed to sales coaching that they reinforce sales coaching training with e-learning, Webinars, podcasts, phones, and other such methods. Some organizations assign coaches to work with sales managers for several months to help them implement their coaching plans and make sales coaching a part of the culture.

The intense focus on sales coaching today is in sharp contrast to just a decade ago, when top salespeople were verbally "knighted" with the title of sales manager and given little or no training in sales coaching to go along with the role. The assumption was that because they were drawn from the ranks of top-performing salespeople, they'd be great sales managers. Unfortunately, too often, this assumption proved wrong. While their sales excellence is a great advantage, it isn't enough. The very skills that make a top performer in sales—the "doer" in them—often get in the way of developing others to "do." Sales managers who are doers like to be in the action, and certainly *in the short run* "doing" has fewer risks, takes less time, and is more comfortable for them. Managers require training and support to help them make the transition from high performing salespeople to developers of the next class of high performers.

As a sales coach, you can learn a lot about your salespeople—each time you coach them. How good are they at assessing a situation? What do they think their obstacles are? What ideas do they have about removing the obstacles? What level of insight about their challenges do they demonstrate? What kind of judgment do they demonstrate? What is their skill level? What is their commitment? What are their attitudes? What kind of effort are they making?

> *Managers require training and support to help them make the transition from high sales performers to developers of the next class of high performers.*

You also learn a lot about yourself. What do you feel about your management role—boss versus coach? Do you want to coach? What are you willing to do to develop yourself?

Sales coaching starts with you taking the leap to make the development of your salespeople your number one priority. With a heart for sales coaching, the skills are the easy part.

You need salespeople who can think on their feet. By using the Developmental Sales Coaching Model, *coaching by asking,* you help them to self-assess and problem-solve and eventually self-coach. There is an old Chinese proverb, "Tell me and I forget. Show me and I remember. Involve me and I understand."

> *"Tell me and I forget. Show me and I remember. Involve me and I understand."*

This e-mail from a sales executive in a multinational company, a leader in its industry, makes the case for Developmental Sales Coaching as priority number one. I received this e-mail as I was writing the second edition of this book:

> A little story for you. I was visiting the Philippines about a month after we did the Richardson Coaching program there. During one of my walk-arounds talking to the salespeople, one of them said to me that she had noticed a marked change in her sales manager, and how much better he was to work for. She said that before he was a very aggressive manager and only asked about results and that salespeople used to talk about how they did not like to work for him. After the coaching program he did the "ask, don't tell" coaching and the salesperson said that he was totally changed and they actually were learning more and enjoyed working for him. Over time I kept an eye on the manager's team performance and they went from 2nd to last performance to 2nd best in a six-month period.

As a sales manager, how much of a priority are you willing to make sales coaching to achieve such impressive and meaningful performance and relationship results?

Now let's focus on *how* to coach.

*Every sales manager has a
sales coaching process.*

Is yours the one you want?

3

Developmental Sales Coaching—The Model

Every sales organization needs salespeople who can analyze situations, think through solutions, use good judgment, and execute successfully. Telling salespeople what to do *may* get them to do that particular thing, but the impact stops there, and an opportunity for real development is lost.

Directing salespeople in what to do rather than eliciting their perceptions and ideas can seem more time-efficient—in the short run. But it comes at a cost. It's a boomerang solution in that salespeople who haven't had to think through what is blocking the desired performance will turn to you as the answer source over and over again. Also, without giving their input, they are much less likely to feel ownership of the solution or a commitment to executing it. Therefore, they are less likely to change. If these reasons weren't compelling enough, you miss the chance to see where they are on the learning or motivational curve. You don't know how they see the situation or whether or not they agree with your solution, or even if they have the skills to carry it out. And without real input from them, you may be working on the wrong obstacle, which will only make the situation worse. Is it skill, knowledge, or will or a combination?

Developmental Sales Coaching is *coaching by asking*—encouraging salespeople to think through their obstacles, share their perceptions, and figure out solutions. Certainly they need your input, and there is no substitute for your being clear on your expectations and goals. And there are times when it is highly appropriate for you to tell. But if *development* (rather than evaluation) of your salespeople is your goal, coaching with questions will produce results and strengthen relationships more effectively and efficiently than any directive you can give.

The Developmental Sales Coaching Model maps out the sales coaching dialogue. It offers a guidepost to help you keep your sales coaching *interactive* and make sure the *responsibility* for development stays where it belongs—with the *salesperson.*

There are two kinds of sales coaching meetings: proactive and reactive. Proactive coaching is planned and scheduled. Reactive coaching is spontaneous and responsive to an immediate problem or opportunity. Proactive Developmental Sales Coaching, because you work on one priority at a time, can usually be completed in *15 minutes.* Reactive coaching meetings are normally shorter—possibly as short as 1 or 2 minutes or as long as 15 minutes or more. Both proactive and reactive sales coaching are essential for any team. The focus in this book is primarily on proactive sales coaching. However, the underlying model is the same for both kinds of coaching, and it applies in face-to-face, phone, 15-minute, corridor, or on-the-go coaching.

Just as there are special movements for picking up something without injuring your back, there are "mechanics" or steps for Developmental Sales Coaching. The steps not only prevent "injury" but also build strength and flexibility.

The Developmental Sales Coaching Model may seem a bi. at first, but the heart and experience you bring to it will make it con. pletely your own. Let's look at the Developmental Sales Coaching Model to help you grow your team—and yourself.

The five steps in the Developmental Sales Coaching are:

Step 1: Connect and Clarify

Step 2: Compare Perceptions

Step 3: Consider Obstacles

Step 4: Construct to Remove Obstacle

Step 5: Commit to Action

In each step there are one to three actions.

Step 1: Connect and Clarify

In Step 1, there are two actions: Rapport and Purpose.

By establishing *rapport* and clarifying the *purpose* of the sales coaching meeting, you will help the salesperson and you ease into the coaching dialogue.

Rapport

There is often a bit of tension when salespeople feel that they are going to be "coached" or get feedback. By paying attention to the human side of the relationship for a few minutes, you can help both the salesperson and you feel more comfortable and open. Even when the sales coaching message is a challenging one to deliver—for example, a lost sale, a relationship in danger, failure to meet goals, and so on—take a moment to establish rapport to help set the tone that you are there to *help* (not evaluate) and that you and the salesperson will be working *together* to improve the situation. While you want to be direct and sincere and you don't want to "beat around the bush," it's almost always appropriate to connect on a personal level. Any genuine comment, whether it's a question about the salesperson's weekend, interest in her squash game, or a discussion of the local team, is appropriate. For example you might ask, "I saw a storm warning on the Weather Channel. How was the flight?" or "I remember when my kids were in fourth grade. How was John's play?"

One of the great things about Developmental Sales Coaching is that it lets you be "hard" on issues without being hard on people. Your goal should be to be *easy* on people but *hard* on issues and measurement.

Purpose

Once you've established rapport for a few moments, clearly state the *purpose* of the coaching. A purpose is an objective with a benefit to the salesperson. Having one objective per Developmental Sales Coaching meeting will help you achieve the best and fastest results and keep the coaching session to a manageable *15 minutes* (approximate) or under. By clarifying the purpose, you set the parameters for the coaching.

> *Your goal should be to be* easy *on people but* hard *on issues and* measurement.

Being clear about the purpose helps the salesperson feel more comfortable by reducing feelings of apprehension. It is very important that you present the purpose in a *neutral, nonjudgmental way*. So whether it's a general comment such as, "Let's debrief the call," or a very specific comment such as, "We agreed to focus on positioning of our price increase, so let's discuss how your meetings with your customers went this week," or "Let's talk about how your effort to cross-sell into your Tier 1 relationships has been going," it should clearly state the purpose.

As you state the purpose, avoid the trap of going too far and revealing your assessment and feelings. Hold back on drawing conclusions or expressing your views. Simple statements such as, "I want to follow up on our talk about your goals for new business and where you are," or, "I would like to discuss the RFP we just learned about from your client" are clear and neutral, not evaluative.

Compare that with evaluative statements such as, "We have a real problem here. You're still not making your new business numbers. Looking at your number of calls in the application, you don't even seem to be trying. How do you explain this?" or, "How can you not be aware your important customer was issuing an RFP? You should have been on top of that and even influenced the RFP. You're supposed to know what's going on with your customers."

If you give your assessment of the situation and/or draw conclusions at the start of the coaching, you are likely to create defensiveness on the part of the salesperson, color the salesperson's own assessment, and send a message that you've already made up your mind about the situation. Judgmental statements turn what should be coaching into evaluation. There is a time for evaluation—but not when you are coaching, and certainly not at the beginning of a coaching meeting.

Judgmental statements won't encourage an open dialogue or strengthen the relationship. While judgmental statements make the purpose clear and are direct, they leave little room for discussion. Most salespeople hearing your perspective are likely to feel that the discussion, for all intents and purposes, is over.

In Step 1, avoid giving your view in any way at all—not even with a general, positive comment such as, "That was a good call" or, "Overall, you handled that client's complaint well." Instead be completely neutral in what you say. Neutral statements create the platform for *asking* salespeople about their perceptions before giving your view.

Your goal in Step 1: connect by establishing rapport and clarify by neutrally getting the topic on the table.

With rapport built and a clear purpose, you are ready to move to Step 2 and learn how the salesperson sees and analyzes the situation.

Step 2: Compare Perceptions

In Step 2, there are two actions: Salesperson's Perceptions, and Your Perceptions and Check.

We have all heard the expression "age before beauty." In sales coaching, it is "salesperson before sales manager."

Salesperson's Perceptions

The key to effective sales coaching can be captured in three words: *they talk first.* Your goal is to get the salesperson to analyze the situation—before you do. This is easier said than done for most sales managers. As a sales manager, you are a born leader. You are action-oriented. You wouldn't have your job if you weren't a leader and a doer. This makes it very tempting for you to want to jump in and take charge to fix the situation. For example, one sales manager with the best of intentions was concerned that a bright young salesperson was spinning her wheels, spending too much time working with an external consultant on what the sales manager viewed as a deal that was a long shot. The sales manager's objective was to help the salesperson become more strategic in deciding where to invest her energy and resources. However, rather than trying to understand why the salesperson saw this as a viable opportunity and was focusing on the consultant rather than getting to the economic decision maker, the sales manager told the salesperson to get to the decision maker or stop spending time and resources on the prospect. He explained why this was important and got her to agree. The salesperson felt unappreciated and frustrated. The sales manager never uncovered that she had neither the confidence nor the skill to actually get to the economic decision maker.

Going into the meeting, the sales manager had an excellent objective. But he had only half the story—his. At the conclusion of a 10-minute discussion, that was still all he had.

Another sales manager described a "real blow-up" with one of his top performers. The sales manager saw a spec sheet in which the salesperson quoted the client a price of $85,000 for a multiple-product package. The sales manager, assuming that the package included three items that were commonly grouped together, was furious that the salesperson would agree to such low pricing. When the salesperson came into the office, rather than probe the situation, he accused the salesperson of giving the services away and threatened to reduce his commission. In fact, as the sales manager soon learned, his assumptions were wrong. The salesperson had sold only the *first part* of the package for $85,000.

> *Your goal is to get the salesperson to analyze the situation—before you do.*

Had the sales manager said, "Gary, I'd like to discuss the pricing of the contract at $85,000, how did you price this?" the sales manager could have avoided straining the relationship. Then, *if* there had been a problem, he could have gone deeper—"What did you base that pricing on? Why? What is your understanding of how we price? What do you suggest doing about this?" and Developmental Sales Coaching could have begun. In fact, had the problem been real, the salesperson might have had to go back to the customer and/or take a reduction in his commission, but he would have felt that his voice had been heard. Moreover, the solution would have been better. Instead, there were assumptions, blame, recriminations, and hard feelings. It bears repeating: Developmental Sales Coaching is hard on issues and soft on people and makes change happen.

The interesting thing is that our research with 1,000 sales managers and our observations of thousands of sales managers show that today about 65 percent of sales managers begin their coaching sessions by *asking a question* (this is up from about 30 percent when I wrote this book in 1996). The problem is, they usually ask *one* question (maybe two), but immediately begin to tell as soon as the salesperson answers. Salespeople, often hoping to get the discussion over with and willing to let the sales manager do all the work, usually answer the question with a short, general response.

If you don't listen carefully and then probe more deeply into the saleperson's answer, you are likely to jump in with your ideas too soon. If you give your perspective too soon, salespeople will likely defend their actions rather than problem-solve with you.

Mac, one of the managers in the National Sales Manager programs at Wharton Aresty Institute, bought into the idea of *they talk first*, but ran into trouble when he volunteered to play the role of the sales coach in a role play:

MAC: Ken, I was very excited about your presentation. You have your product knowledge down pat. It seems like you went through the presentation *with* your peers before the meeting to prepare.

I was, however, *very* disappointed with some aspects. I've discussed the need to probe more with you before. I *would have expected* that you would have *corrected* this problem. What you said about our offering was pretty generic. Someone with your experience should be able to map out the customer's needs, link our offering with those needs, and quantify value specifically to what's important to the customer. We've agreed that it is important to involve the customer and show value to the customer to get him to act. I *explained* how important this was.

Mac was direct, clear, articulate, and honest. He even started with strengths. But when the sales managers in the Wharton program were asked to give positive feedback to Mac, the best they could offer half-jokingly was, "He refrained from a direct blow to the head."

Before the role play, when we set objectives for the workshop, the number one goal of the sales managers in the program was to "motivate" their salespeople—other than financially. After the role play, they all agreed that Mac's approach would not accomplish the goal of motivation or have much of an impact on improving Ken's performance.

Then the people in the group had a change of heart. They decided that since Mac had already given this feedback to Ken, Mac's approach was in fact appropriate. Using the magic of the classroom "time machine," we let Mac role-play that *first* coaching meeting where he had given the feedback for the first time. The results were revealing. The first meeting was a repeat of this one—with Mac doing all the talking, assessing, and so on. The sales managers at the training session clearly saw that the process that Mac used ("telling") was not the result of circumstances. Everyone agreed that Mac needed to change his coaching style—except Mac.

One participant saw a way to get through to him. "Mac, you said to Ken, 'It's important to involve customers and show value to them to motivate them to act.' How would you apply that to Ken to get him to change?" Bingo. Mac squinted and said, "I guess I pretty much shut him down and didn't help him." Mac acknowledged that he hadn't followed the model and that he really hadn't asked questions to understand how the salesperson saw the call. Nor had he given balanced feedback. He asked to try it again with the objective of getting Ken to self-access. With some coaching, the results of this role play were very different:

Connect

MAC: It's been a long day, and they certainly had a lot of questions. Let's take a few minutes to debrief the call. What are your thoughts?

Compare

KEN: I think it went well. I felt ready to handle the questions, and I saw a lot of nodding heads. What do you think?

MAC: Yes, I agree the nodding heads were a good sign. As you think about the call, what other specific strengths and also areas for improvement did you see?

KEN: Well, I think they know we have a good solution. You saw that I did a lot of the talking, but I had a lot of information to cover. They're not that sophisticated, as you could see from their questions. I think I answered the questions well.

MAC: That's true. Clearly you know your product. What else did you observe?

KEN: From here on it's just follow up. They'll be making a decision in two weeks, and I will call my contact tomorrow morning after she meets with her team and get a follow-up e-mail out. I know they are talking to one other competitor tomorrow, and I'll try to get feedback on that too.

MAC: That sounds good. In the past we've talked about the need to ask more questions as a way to customize our solution. You mentioned that you did a lot of the talking because you had a lot of information to cover and they're not very sophisticated. How else might you have handled that without doing so much of the talking? *(Encouraging the salesperson to analyze the call and think of other possibilities and options.)*

KEN: Well, I guess I could have asked if they had any questions after I covered each part of our solution. It did feel like I was going on for a little too long.

MAC: Ken, it's good that you were aware of that. What . . . ?

Mac was well on his way to understanding Ken's perspective and helping Ken broaden that perspective, remove the obstacle to probing and customizing, and change his behavior.

By asking questions and probing further into the answers that salespeople give, you can help them analyze their performance and *consider other options*. It takes discipline and patience to ask questions and listen to salespeople.

Regardless of your first question, a rule of thumb is to ask at least *two more questions* before giving your perceptions. For example, if a salesperson says, "The specialist just won't make time for me. So how am I supposed to get him in to see my customers?" acknowledge the salesperson's feelings and ask questions to help the salesperson analyze the situation: "I can see how that can be a problem. Why do you think he's not making time for you?" "What might another possibility be?" "How are you approaching him?"

By asking questions, you will learn so much: where the salesperson is on the learning curve, and how good her insights, skills, and judgment are. Most importantly, you are getting information that will help you direct your coaching and give very specific feedback. Probing also helps you maximize the use of your coaching time because you get to the issues more quickly.

By asking questions rather than telling, you show salespeople that you value their perceptions, and you foster a collaborative approach that leads to buy-in. Even though in many situations you will feel that you have the answers or a best guess based on your experience and knowledge as well as the data you have and your feelings, hold back, ask questions, listen, and drill down into the answers. Help them learn to analyze, solve problems, self-assess, and self-coach.

Coaching by asking is different from the traditional Expert Coaching Model. In the Expert Coaching Model, sales managers take the responsibility for assessing the situation, identifying the obstacle, and removing it. The problem with this is that it is the salespeople who have to implement the solution. Whether or not salespeople are committed to the actions or have the skills to make the change is unknown. With the Expert Coaching Model, you are the answer man or woman. In today's world of change and with today's workforce, this role is almost impossible to fill.

Collaboration is the way to achieve the best results. Developmental Sales Coaching is based on the Resource Model, which positions you as a part of a development continuum: "I know. You know. Others know. Let's figure it out and know more." Of course you are essential to adding value—but part of that value is encouraging salespeople to think.

Your Perceptions and Check

Once salespeople have analyzed their performance and shared their perceptions of the situation, then it's your turn to share *your perceptions*. This is when you give *your feedback*. Your job is to be *honest* and *clear* as you describe your perceptions of the salesperson's *strengths* and *areas for improvement*. Limit your feedback to one priority at a time. Use examples so that he understands what you are

> Collaboration is the way to achieve the best results.

talking about. Start by *acknowledging* what the salesperson has said and *reinforcing* any strengths and areas for improvement that you agree with to build common ground.

Be specific and give positives *before* you mention areas for improvement. You may say something like, "I agree with you on . . . (acknowledge). I'd like to share my perceptions. I thought . . . was really strong, and I think the customer liked it when you said . . . (strengths). I also saw opportunities for you to do more . . . and . . .; for example, . . . (areas for improvement and examples and impact)." Or, "Here's what I think: when the customer said . . . and you . . ., I thought you could have. . . ." Or "I agree with you; you tried to move the delivery date, and that may have caused the confusion with the customer. I also think that by not checking the date with . . ., you risked . . ., which caused us to disappoint the customer and lose credibility with her."

By giving both strengths and areas for improvement, you show that you have a balanced view. The more specific the feedback you give, the clearer the picture you paint for the salesperson will be. Specific examples will help him know what you are talking about. Use examples that describe the behavior as well as show the impact of the behavior.

For example, "I agree that you really knew your products and were well prepared. I also agree that it would have helped if you had asked if she had any questions after you covered each part of our solution. Even before this, I think there was a need to ask about her objectives before you started to describe our solution so that you could tailor the solution to her language and needs and be more persuasive. For example, when you talked about our . . ., you could have tied it to their. . . . I'm concerned that our proposal will be generic. What do you think about the need to ask questions up front?"

The purpose of giving feedback is to broaden a salesperson's perspective. *Everyone has blind spots, and your salespeople need your view (an outside view) to improve.* If they knew a better way to perform, they would most likely be doing it. Feedback gives salespeople a lens that lets them see what they otherwise wouldn't see.

Once your and the salesperson's perceptions are on the table, ask the salesperson for feedback on what you've said before going any further. Sometimes both perceptions will be perfectly aligned. More often than not, however, there will be some differences between how you and the salesperson see the situation. Your job then is to gain agreement or to identify and deal with the differences.

> *Everyone has blind spots, and your salespeople need your view (an outside view) to improve.*

This juncture is not dissimilar to going out in the morning and finding snow on the windshield of your car. Regardless of what kind of car you have or how good a driver you are, you are not going anywhere until the snow is removed from the windshield. The "removal of the snow" in sales coaching is getting agreement that there is an obstacle to remove. Do this by simply asking the salesperson how she feels about your feedback. If the salesperson accepts and agrees with your feedback, the snow is off; turn on the engine and move to Step 3. If there is not agreement, there is some work to do.

Acknowledge the salesperson's resistance and probe to see what is behind it. Most often you will be able to work things out and gain agreement. When you can't get agreement, if the point is not important and is something that you can live with, you may agree to disagree or, more likely, agree to live with the salesperson's perspective for a limited period of time to give his idea a chance. If it is something

> *Feedback gives salespeople a lens that lets them see what they otherwise wouldn't see.*

that you cannot live with, as a last resort you can use your authority and demand compliance. Since many salespeople will do what they want to anyway, it makes a lot more sense to work to get their buy-in, and a helpful way to do this is to ask more questions to help them think it through.

One sales manager said that it is very rare for him to have to use his "The train has left the station, and it is going in one direction— either you are on or you're off" speech. He uses this as infrequently as possible because he realizes that he'll get compliance at best. He works to get buy-in.

Step 3: Consider Obstacles

Step 3 is made up of two actions: Salesperson's Perception of the Obstacle, and Your Perception of the Obstacle and Check. Spend up to 30 percent of your coaching time here.

With perceptions on the table and agreement about the need for an improvement, you are ready to help the salesperson consider what is blocking the desired behavior. In Step 3, continue to use the "they talk first" strategy. Ask the salesperson to identify the obstacle.

Salesperson's Perception of the Obstacle

Identifying the obstacle may seem like a mystery. That is exactly what one sales manager called it. But it is a mystery that usually can be solved quickly if you ask the simple question, "What do you think the obstacle to your . . . is?" and you fill in the desired behavior.

By asking this question, you help salespeople think about what is blocking them from the preferred behavior or the desired results. For example, you can ask a salesperson who has agreed that he is targeting the wrong kind of customers and that there is a need to change, "What do you think is the obstacle to your prospecting customers that meet . . . criteria?" Another example would be, "Ken, what do you think is the obstacle to asking questions to understand the customer's needs before getting into our capabilities?"

Listen, acknowledge, and drill down until the salesperson has, as much as possible, thought through *what is blocking the successful behavior.* You almost always will have to repeat your question and ask two or three drill-down questions to help salespeople analyze fully. Say, "That is one possibility. What's another possibility?" or "Why do you feel that way?" to help them get unstuck.

Your Perception of the Obstacle and Check

Acknowledge the salesperson's analysis of the obstacle and give your perspective to reinforce, reshape, or add value to her thinking as a way to share your knowledge and experience. For example, if a salesperson feels that the only obstacle to identifying new business is that her territory is saturated, you can discuss referrals and networking with her and check for agreement: "What do you think about what I've said?" or "What do you think about getting referrals and networking as a way to identify qualified prospects?" If the salesperson accepts your ideas, move on to Step 4; if not, probe to find out why as a way to reach agreement.

Step 4: Construct to Remove Obstacle

In Step 4 there are three actions: Salesperson Removes the Obstacle, Your Value Add and Check, and Practice. Step 4 is the heart of sales coaching. Spend about half of your coaching meeting time here.

Salesperson Removes the Obstacle

Once the key obstacle(s) is identified and agreed upon, keep the responsibility on the salesperson to remove it by asking questions such

as, "What do you think you can do to . . . (remove the obstacle)?"—
for example, "What do you suggest doing to help you get in to see
prospects who are more in line with our target market?" This is the
part of sales coaching where Richardson research and experience show
that many sales managers slip into a directive versus collaborative
mode. But if you ask questions here you will find it very eye-opening
in understanding how your salespeople think and what they know.
When you ask a question such as, "Well, what do you think you should
do?" you'll sometimes find that their solutions exceed your expectations in how strategic and creative they are. You also may be disappointed by a lack of insight or motivation. Either way, you have
valuable information that will guide you in your coaching.

When one coach in a call center asked a salesperson who missed
a cross-selling opportunity what she could do to remove the obstacle to identifying cues for cross-selling, she didn't simply make a
commitment to review her cross-selling guide, listen for cues, and
take notes in upcoming calls. She asked her coach to listen in while
she reconnected to the customer with whom she had missed the
cross-selling opportunity. Her call started with, "Mrs. . . ., I realized
after we spoke that you mentioned . . ., and I wanted to see if we
could help with that. May I ask you . . .?" and ended with the sale of
two additional products and a thank-you not only from the sales rep
to the customer but from the customer to her. Another salesperson
recognized that her obstacle to cross-selling was her fear of not being
able to answer customer questions. When asked what she thought
she could do to correct this, she suggested reviewing her relationship plans for key customers with the various specialists to get ideas
for questions to ask, what to listen for, and what to position.

If a salesperson has difficulty thinking of ideas for removing a
particular obstacle, encourage him to try harder before you offer
suggestions. Ask what the desired outcome would be, and then ask
for options to achieve that outcome. If the salesperson truly is unable

to suggest an idea, give your perspective, but only as a starting point. Once you offer an idea, ask the salesperson how he feels about it to get him to assess it and buy into it.

> *Encourage him to try harder before you offer suggestions.*

Here is an example of a revealing coaching session in which a sales manager asked a salesperson for her ideas on how to resolve a customer situation in which a major customer was upset about a late delivery:

SALES COACH: . . . called me and was very upset about. . . . What will you do at this point?

SALESPERSON: I'll call him first thing Monday morning. *(It was late Friday afternoon.)*

SALES COACH: Why Monday? *(Thinking "Monday! How much of a priority is this? What about now?")*

SALESPERSON: There really isn't anything we can do today.

SALES COACH: Why do you say that?

SALESPERSON: Well, it's late, and there is no way to get that corrected today.

SALES COACH: That's true. What about the customer?

SALESPERSON: I could let him know I'm aware of the problem and I'm working on it.

SALES COACH: I agree because . . . What do you think about doing that?

Under the Expert Coaching Model, the sales manager would not have asked for the salesperson's solution but would simply have told the salesperson what to do ("Call the customer now. Explain . . .").

This would have solved the customer's problem then and there, but the salesperson's apparent lack of judgment, lack of urgency, and lack of responsiveness would have gone undetected and uncorrected. The coach not only helped address a customer problem but also gained tremendous insight into the salesperson. Marching orders at best solve the immediate problem, but not the next one.

Your Value Add and Check

Most of the time salespeople are able to suggest ideas for removing their obstacles. It is also likely that you will be able to add value with additional input.

By asking salespeople how to remove the obstacle, you get a clear picture of where the salespeople are in their development, and you can use that information to add your ideas and help them improve.

Acknowledge the salesperson's ideas, then add value with your knowledge and experience, and check for agreement. For example, if the salesperson doesn't suggest calling the customer that day to let him know that she is aware of the problem and is working on it, you would position the need to get to the customer immediately, particularly before a weekend so that the customer is not upset all weekend, and check for agreement.

Practice

Once options and ideas are on the table, it is often helpful to take a few minutes to make sure that the salesperson can confidently and successfully execute what has been decided. This often requires putting on your teaching cap, whether you practice together, demonstrate, role-play, brainstorm, review, plan, agree to observe, make an assignment (such as generating a list of names of centers of influence such as CPAs), or engage in any other kind of support you can provide.

By practicing, one coach helped a new salesperson develop a "close" and the confidence to ask for the business. The company used what it called a "soft sell" close: instead of being able to ask for and get a "hard order," its salespeople sought a commitment for future business. Unaccustomed to this kind of selling, the new hire was underperforming, and his job was at risk. After working together on developing a close, the salesperson role-played this close: "We want to support you with our research and will be as competitive as possible. I will keep in touch with you. You mentioned that you are expecting to do . . . this month. Given what we talked about and our . . ., I'd like to call you each morning… And when you are in the market with this, will you give us an even shot?" This close worked wonders, according to the salesperson, and saved his job.

Step 5: Commit to Action

Step 5 is made up of three actions: Action Step, Summarize, and Encouragement.

Developmental Sales Coaching is about incremental growth, working on one thing at a time, and taking small but essential steps to make big gains. Those big gains are achieved by gaining commitment to a few specific *action steps* with a *time frame for completion*.

While it is important to leave the responsibility for implementing the action steps with the salespeople, commitment is mutual. Your commitment is in the form of support (not doing for). Support can be coaching, encouragement, follow-up, noticing incremental progress or problems, or actions on your part such as calling a specialist to let him know that he can expect a call from the salesperson and encouraging the specialist to be helpful.

Action Step

Keep the responsibility for the action step with the salesperson. Once you have ideas on the table ask the salesperson, "Now that we . . ., what are you thinking of doing?" Clarify who, what, and when.

For example, one salesperson suggested as her action steps signing up for the e-learning product knowledge series available through her sales force automation system, contacting specialists before each call to review her customers' needs, and brainstorming opportunities with the specialists on how to penetrate her key relationships. She also agreed to identify and close two cross-selling opportunities over a one-month period.

In situations where you feel that the action steps salespeople suggest are not appropriate, you can probe and give your guidance. If a salesperson suggests an action step that is outside his control—for example, getting an administrative assistant or being sent to a training program—while the idea may have merit and may be a *part* of the solution, put the responsibility back on the salesperson by asking what he will change that is *within his immediate control.* And most importantly, don't allow the solution to be something delegated to you to do, such as your making the customer call *for* the salesperson, unless, of course, you are demonstrating the call and then observing the next. Ask, "What can *you* do *now* that is within *your control?*"

One of the goals of sales coaching is to help your salespeople become "internal" so that they believe that they are a factor in what happens to them, rather than being "external" and feeling like a victim—whining and blaming others. In doing this, you are helping them do what successful people in all walks of life do—attribute their success in great part to what *they* do. External people, on the other hand, believe that things *happen* to them. They attribute their lot in life to things such as "being in the right place," "whom you know," "luck," "the better territory," "being 'X,' not 'Y,'" and so on. A part of sales coaching is helping salespeople believe that they are in control of their results.

Summarize

Make sure that the salesperson and you are in agreement about expectations. At the end of the coaching meeting, ask the salesperson to summarize what was decided.

> *A part of sales coaching is helping salespeople believe that they are in control of their results.*

You might say, "Jim, could you summarize what you will do from here?" Listen for output and time frame. Here are some examples:

"For my next call with . . ., I'll prepare strategic questions and in the call continue to ask them until we understand their objectives and our competitive position. I'll leave you a voice mail tomorrow after the call to. . . ."

"By the end of the month, close these two deals with signed contracts."

"Meet with my three top-tier customers within the next 2.5 weeks to arrange . . . and meet with you to review progress against cross-selling objectives at the end of the month on. . . ."

"Before each of my seven sales calls next week, I'll check out the customers' organizational charts and identify possible areas for expansion. I'll call my contacts and ask them for introductions and find out as much as I can about what is going on. I want to get at least three introductions by the middle of the month. And we'll take a look at how this goes on the 18th."

"Starting Monday, I'll visit with six customers a day, up from the three I've been visiting, and enter the data into the SFA."

The action steps must be measurable, observable, and time-sensitive so that the salesperson and you can assess progress. If the salesperson's summary is missing any parts, you have the opportunity to edit as needed so that expectations are clear.

Encouragement

At the end of each coaching meeting, reinforce your support and confidence in the salesperson. Cheerlead by wrapping up the coaching with words of encouragement. A few words from you—when genuine—like, "I know you can do it. I'm here if you have questions or need me!" mean so much.

Coaching Dialogue Examples 1 and 2

As you read the following two examples of coaching dialogues, notice that in the first example, the sales manager asks questions, but without much success. Compare that with the second example, in which the sales manager uses questions in the spirit and form of the Developmental Sales Coaching Model:

Background: The salesperson has lost his last two deals. The feedback from one of the customers was, "They just didn't connect." The salesperson has strong technical skills but seems to be weak in relating to customers and colleagues. The sales manager has discussed the need to strengthen rapport skills with him previously. They are now debriefing a team call in which the development objective was to focus on rapport building.

Example 1

Dialogue	Critique
SALES MANAGER: How do you think the call went?	Good start in that the sales manager asked for salesperson's perception before giving his, but the sales manager did not build rapport or clarify the purpose.
SALESPERSON: Great. I'm confident we're going to get the business.	Brief, general response.
SALES MANAGER: Well, do you remember the conversation we had after our last call, when I mentioned that I thought you needed to spend some time on rapport?	Closed-ended, leading question rather than a question to elicit the salesperson's thoughts on strengths and areas for improvement.
SALESPERSON: Vividly!	Sarcasm.
SALES MANAGER: Do you see any similarities between that conversation and this call?	Closed-ended leading question to prompt the salesperson to agree rather than to gain the salesperson's perspective.
SALESPERSON: Yes.	Brief response.
SALES MANAGER: Well, what are they?	Good question, but asked with a grilling tone.
SALESPERSON: That rapport stuff. I think it's a little hokey. It can't help us make the numbers.	Brief, frank response from the salesperson.

Dialogue	Critique
SALES MANAGER: Well, let me ask you this: do you think rapport could have helped you do a better job?	Closed-ended leading question to prompt agreement rather than probing to understand why the salesperson thinks rapport is hokey and won't help in making the numbers. The sales manager is communicating her feelings of dissatisfaction about the call.
SALESPERSON: No. I think she'd ramble. I'm not convinced that rapport works, and I hadn't much time.	Defensive, brief, frank response.
SALES MANAGER: If you look at our corporate policy and other successful salespeople, you'll see that is how we work here. For future calls, I want you to take time on rapport. Relationships are important here.	The sales manager uses her authority; she has not identified the obstacle, removed it, or gained buy-in.

This "coaching" session actually happened. How would you rate it? On the positive side, the sales manager did make an attempt to coach with questions. Unfortunately, she used leading questions aimed at promoting her views rather than helping the salesperson analyze the situation or identify and remove the obstacles in his path.

How you probe sends a message. Leading questions generally discourage dialogue, prompt defensive responses, or seek to force an agreement that may or may not get carried out.

Let's look at the coaching session using the Developmental Sales Coaching Model and mind-set.

Example 2
Connect and Clarify

Dialogue	Critique
SALES COACH: That was really quite a call, wasn't it? She's quite direct. This customer really has got us all running around.	Good rapport, empathy
SALESPERSON: She sure has.	

Compare Perceptions

SALES COACH: Yeah. How do you think the call went?	Perception question.
SALESPERSON: Really good. She sees that we have the best solution. I'm pretty confident based on her comment at the end.	Clear, brief response.
SALES COACH: I agree. She sees the value. You know, Bill, at our last session, we discussed rapport. Now while we're fresh from our call, I'd like to specifically look at this. So how do you think you handled rapport?	Acknowledgment. Clear, specific, neutral *purpose* to follow up on previous coaching dialogue. Neutral probe to gain the salesperson's perceptions.

Dialogue	Critique
SALESPERSON: I think she's fine. I think the call was great! I'm confident we're going to get the business.	Avoided the coach's question.
SALES COACH: That would be terrific! It's a good piece of business. What in particular leads you to think we'll get it?	The sales coach acknowledges to continue to build rapport by reinforcing common ground and continues to probe and asks a drill-down question.
SALESPERSON: Well, she said to call her tomorrow. She was also getting into specs. It sounds like she's made a decision. I also feel I really answered her questions, and she wants a proposal.	Good insight, analysis.
SALES COACH: Yes, these are good signals, and you know your stuff. I liked how you explained. . . . It was very clear.	Reinforced agreement, reinforced positives.
SALESPERSON: Thanks. I'm really excited about this opportunity.	Encouraged.
SALES COACH: Good. I can tell. We discussed your working on rapport. How do you think you did in that area?	The sales coach *repeated* the question to get the salesperson to focus on the coaching objective of strengthening his rapport skills.

(continued on next page)

Example 2 (continued)
Compare Perceptions

Dialogue	Critique
SALESPERSON: That rapport stuff. I think it's hokey. It can't help us make the numbers, and I'm ready to do a proposal.	Brief, frank response.
SALES COACH: Hmm. Why do you feel that way about rapport?	The sales coach acknowledged and probed to help the salesperson analyze his approach and his performance.
SALESPERSON: She'd jump at it and start rambling, and we'd never get to tell our story.	Salesperson's analysis/ perception.
SALES COACH: That's one possibility. What's another possibility?	The sales coach is helping the salesperson consider other options and broaden his perspective.
SALESPERSON: Well, it could make her a bit more comfortable with us.	The salesperson is gaining new perspectives.
SALES COACH: I agree. What impact could that have?	The sales coach is asking drill-down question and asks the salesperson for impact.
SALESPERSON: Well, she'd probably open up a bit and feel that I was interested in her and not just the sale. But we had a lot to cover.	The salesperson is considering other possibilities but is still a bit defensive.

Dialogue	Critique
SALES COACH: I think that's true. How important is it for her to feel that we are interested in her?	The sales coach continues probing.
SALESPERSON: I guess it is pretty important in getting her to want to do business with us. We did have only 30 minutes.	Salesperson's agreement.
SALES COACH: I know we had a lot to cover and we had only 30 minutes. Let's explore the connection between helping customers feel more comfortable and buying. I think you're right that she would feel we were interested in her. I've found that people buy from people they like and that taking a few minutes to build rapport and learn about them on a personal level to show your interest in them helps you connect and encourages them to share information we can use to customize our solution. What do you think about rapport being important?	The sales coach gives his perception, adds value with feedback, and checks for agreement.

(continued on next page)

Example 2 (continued)
Compare Perceptions

Dialogue	Critique
SALESPERSON: I'm afraid she'd see right through it if it's not genuine. I'm not good at rapport. I sort of know I should work on my rapport building. I really don't have a lot in common with her—at all. I'm young enough to be her son.	The salesperson is opening up and further analyzing his performance and sales approach and coach identifies resistance.

Consider Obstacles

SALES COACH: With some customers, building rapport can be more challenging. I agree about the need to be genuine and also about your working on your rapport skills. *What do you think is stopping you (obstacle) from developing your rapport skills and finding things in common so that your rapport feels more genuine?*	The sales coach acknowledges and asks the obstacle question.
SALESPERSON: I guess I just didn't take the time. Nothing came to me *naturally*, and there was no obvious connection.	The salesperson is identifying the obstacle—lack of preparation for rapport, not picking up on cues, and expecting rapport to always come naturally.

Dialogue	Critique
SALES COACH: In thinking about the meeting, what might you have done in advance to make up for the lack of *natural* connection?	The sales coach is asking the salesperson how to remove the obstacle.
SALESPERSON: I could have asked her a few questions about herself and also picked up on the two trophies on her shelf. I did notice them.	The salesperson is coming up with options.
SALES COACH: I agree that questions are one of the best ways to build personal rapport. And office cues are also very useful, when used with tact. What else?	The sales coach acknowledges and probes.
SALESPERSON: I'm not sure. You know, I could have asked my contact in operations, where she used to work, about her to get some background.	The salesperson is coming up with more ideas to remove the obstacle.
SALES COACH: These are all really great ideas. We often expect rapport to be natural—and sometimes it is—but it usually takes preparation. Your idea about the contact in operations is very important, especially if they knew each other. You might also check her bio on the company Web site, or even Google her. What do you think about doing this?	The sales coach is encouraging, acknowledging, adding value, and checking for agreement.

(continued on next page)

Example 2 (continued)
Consider Obstacles

Dialogue	Critique
SALESPERSON: I hadn't really thought about preparing for rapport, but you're right—it's a good idea. Why not? I can do it.	The salesperson agrees with the action steps discussed.

Construct to Remove Obstacle

SALES COACH: I know you can. What do you think you can do to help build your rapport skills?	The sales coach is finding out if the salesperson has the skill and the knowledge to implement the action steps.
SALESPERSON: It seems obvious now. I could have planned some ways to build rapport. I could ask her how she likes her role in this division after being in operations downtown, and even mentioned my contact there and asked about the trophies on the shelf.	Salesperson generates ideas.
SALES COACH: So what do you think you can do to connect with her?	Sales coach continues to probe.
SALESPERSON: I have a follow-up phone call set for tomorrow. I'll call my contact in operations and then use that to ask about	Salesperson continues to generate ideas.

Dialogue	Critique
her new role. I'll even Google her before the call.	
SALES COACH: Good ideas. How do you feel about practicing with me?	Sales coach offers option to practice.
SALESPERSON: I'll give it a try. It will help if we work on a few rapport questions together.	

(Practice and Feedback)

Commit to Action

SALES COACH: So why don't you summarize what you plan to do?	Sales coach asks salesperson to summarize.
SALESPERSON: I'll call her tomorrow and let you know in an e-mail how it goes. It seems so obvious. I also have a call with Tim tomorrow morning; I feel we just haven't clicked, and it's probably my fault. I'll try this with him.	Salesperson summarizes and applies learning to another customer situation.
SALES COACH: That sounds great! I know you'll be successful. I'm here if you want to debrief the call or if you need to talk about this further.	Sales coach encourages.
SALESPERSON: I'll drop you an e-mail. Thanks!	

As a result of working together for a matter of 10 or so minutes, this salesperson is likely to be more confident and effective in building rapport with customers and colleagues—and in strengthening and penetrating relationships.

If you are thinking that salespeople should be able to figure things out for themselves, some may be able to. But most people need an outside perspective to help them improve. An example of this is a seasoned, high-performing salesperson who was sorely lacking in rapport skills. When a peer in a seminar suggested that he simply ask his customers about their weekend, he wrote the idea down and was proud to report that by using this idea, he was enjoying getting to know his customers on a more personal level and executing bigger trades.

"They Talk First" Model

Coaching by asking rather than *coaching by telling* boils down to a philosophy of what is the best way to help your salespeople learn—and change. John Locke, the seventeenth-century English philosopher, believed that people are born *tabula rasa*—a "blank slate"—and that they must be instructed in everything. Plato, the ancient Greek philosopher, held the opposite view; he believed that people are born knowing everything they need to know. He saw the role of the teacher as one who evoked this innate knowledge through questions. Developmental Sales Coaching follows the thinking of Plato. By *coaching by asking*, you help salespeople draw on what they know, you help foster buy-in because they are more open when they feel they have been heard, and you accelerate improvement. *Coaching by asking* not only removes the current obstacle but teaches salespeople how to remove other obstacles themselves.

It is a collaborative process. Your role as sales coach in this collaboration is essential. You need to initiate it and be a role model for openness to feedback. Your expertise and value are essential to shaping, molding, refining, and building on the ideas your salespeople offer. Optimal learning occurs when the learner is actively involved, and in coaching that means being involved in identifying and removing the obstacle. You as the coach benefit too—not only will your coaching have more impact, but you will never stop learning.

> *Coaching by asking teaches salespeople how to remove other obstacles themselves.*

The flow of the Developmental Sales Coaching dialogue follows a consistent pattern throughout the steps. Whether it is Step 2, Step 3, or Step 4 a pattern is repeated:

- The salesperson talks first.

- The coach gives feedback/adds value.

- The coach checks for agreement.

Steps 3, "Consider Obstacles," and 4, "Construct to Remove Obstacle," are the heart of Developmental Sales Coaching. Spend 80 percent of your coaching time there.

The measure of how effectively you execute the model can be answered by a simple question: "Who did all the work?" Using the model will help you keep the responsibility for development where it belongs—with the salespeople. The process of *coaching by asking* will become second nature—it will move you from being the answer man or woman to being the resource your salespeople know they can turn to to be heard and helped.

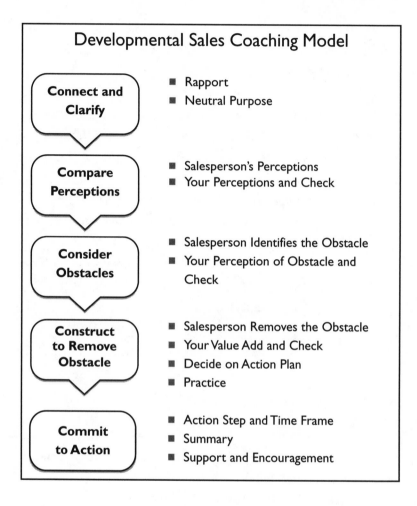

Developmental Sales Coaching Model

Connect and Clarify
- Rapport
- Neutral Purpose

Compare Perceptions
- Salesperson's Perceptions
- Your Perceptions and Check

Consider Obstacles
- Salesperson Identifies the Obstacle
- Your Perception of Obstacle and Check

Construct to Remove Obstacle
- Salesperson Removes the Obstacle
- Your Value Add and Check
- Decide on Action Plan
- Practice

Commit to Action
- Action Step and Time Frame
- Summary
- Support and Encouragement

Developmental Sales Coaching—
Sales Coach's Debriefing

Sales Coaching Objective: _____

Salesperson:_____ Date: _____

	Yes	**No**	**Debriefing Notes**

Connect and Clarify
- Rapport
- Connect with the Purpose

**Compare
Perceptions**
- Salesperson's
  Perceptions
- Your Perceptions
  and Check

**Consider
Obstacles**
- Salesperson Identifies
  the Obstacle
- Your Perception of
  Obstacle and Check

**Construct to
Remove Obstacle**
- Salesperson
  Removes Obstacle
- Your Value Add and Check
- Decide on Action Plan
- Practice

Commit to Action
- Action Step and Time
  Frame
- Summary
- Support and
  Encouragement

*T*he power of sales coaching is

in the questions you ask.

4

Developmental Sales Coaching—The Skills

The six critical skills needed for selling—presence, relating, questioning, listening, positioning, and checking—are the same communication skills needed for coaching.

If one of the critical skills had to be singled out as the core skill of Developmental Sales Coaching, it would be questioning. *Coaching by questioning* takes patience and skill, and the ability to phrase questions in a way that helps salespeople think through the issues and answer openly.

Not all questions are equal. By knowing how to pose questions that encourage an open dialogue, you can help salespeople analyze the situation, remove obstacles, find solutions, and learn to self-assess.

The Developmental Sales Coaching process often requires increasing the number and intensity of the questions you ask. The following questioning skills encourage salespeople to think and open up.

Ask Drill-Down Questions

Because salespeople frequently tend to respond with general, brief answers when they are asked for their perceptions, it's important to probe further into what they say to encourage them to broaden their ideas and possibilities. Asking the simple question "why?" can be very revealing. It stimulates dialogue, helps the salesperson analyze further, and gives you insights and direction for your coaching. For example:

> SALESPERSON: It went well. We have everyone's support except Joe's. But I think we'll get the contract anyway.

> SALES COACH: I agree. It looks good for us. What's the obstacle with Joe? . . . What have you tried to do to win his support? . . . What makes you think we'll get the contract anyway?

Ask Directive Questions

When you want to put a coaching topic on the table, ask a question that focuses the salesperson's attention on the specific area that you want to explore. For example, if you feel that a proposal was not acceptable (because of typos, incomplete response, or content errors), ask, "What do you think of the quality of the proposal?" or, "How do you think our proposal stacked up against . . .?"

It's important to probe further into what they say to encourage them to broaden their ideas and possibilities.

If you think there is a gap in the salesperson's product knowledge, ask, "How comfortable are you with your understanding of X product?"

then drill down further with questions such as, "Which of your clients do you think have a need for this product?" If a salesperson was inactive during a team call, ask, "How do you feel about your participation in the call?" Once you hear the salesperson's perceptions, you are in a better position to give yours and to direct your coaching.

Ask Neutral Questions

With neutral questions, you get the salesperson's perspectives without revealing your bias or position. The opposite of a neutral question is a leading question that is phrased to promote a particular response and/or color the salesperson's response. A leading question such as, "Don't you think your silence during the call weakened the way the customer sees our team?" makes your feelings known and signals to the salesperson what you want to hear, not an open dialogue. Leading questions often provoke defensiveness and risk closing down communication. And even if salespeople concede, they may not agree.

Ask Open-Ended Questions

By force of habit, many people ask closed-ended questions (questions that begin with words such as *are* or *do* and elicit yes or no responses). Open-ended questions (questions that begin with words such as *what* or *how*) stimulate a more complete response. Make an effort to use open-ended questions to help your salespeople answer thoughtfully and fully.

Questioning Techniques

There are several questioning techniques that you can use to motivate salespeople to answer more completely and also make both you and the salespeople more comfortable with the question. As you pose questions, lead into them with:

■ *Acknowledgment.* Before you ask a question, preface the question by acknowledging what the salesperson has said.

SALES COACH: *I agree he's a talker.* What do you think you could do to make sure you have time to make your presentation without interrupting him?

■ *Positive reinforcement.* Introduce your question with a compliment or agreement to maintain rapport and encourage participation in the dialogue.

SALES COACH: *That sounds like a great plan.* What are your time frames?

■ *Benefits to the salesperson.* Motivate the salesperson to respond frankly by showing what's in it for her.

SALES COACH: *Since I know Bob and maybe I can give some insight,* tell me what you've done so far to try to get to him.

■ *Trading information.* Exchange information, to give so that you can get.

SALES COACH: *I remember once getting a question like that.* How do you think you handled Dan's question?

The Power of Questions

I witnessed the amazing power of questions in a seminar with a group of sales managers whose industry and organization were going though a massive shake-up. We all learned the power of repetition in uncovering obstacles. The assignment was to ask the same person one question three times. Sales Manager 1 asked Sales Manager 2 the question, "Do you like your job?" Sales Manager 2 answered, "Yes. Yes, I do." Sales Manager 1 repeated the question. This time, Sales Manager 2 responded, "Well, basically I do. I have autonomy, and I like the people I work with. I like my work." Sales Manager 1 then asked the same question again. Sales Manager 2 said, "That's enough." But Sales Manager 1 persisted, and Sales Manager 2 responded: "Yes, I like my job, but I'm not challenged. I used to feel different. Now I do the same things over and over. How many line sheets can you look at? . . . Every day I. . . . I would like to have some passion back in my work—feel excitement again."

What the group experienced was the power of taking the time and having the patience to question and listen and what it takes to help people open up. As the question was repeated, each response was more complete, more thoughtful, more honest, and more meaningful. An obstacle was on the table, and the sales manager took the opportunity to begin to remove it.

Resolving Objections

As you know, customers are not the only ones who object. You're likely to encounter some resistance from your salespeople as you coach them. They may object to the process of *coaching by asking,* or they may disagree about the objective, obstacle, or solution.

Objections to the Developmental Sales Coaching Process

Some salespeople may take exception to being asked to play such a big role in the coaching by questioning process and having to identify and remove the obstacle. When this happens, the subject of being coached becomes the topic of the coaching. Sales managers who believe in the value of *coaching by asking* are able to remain firm.

SALESPERSON: You're the sales manager. Tell me what you want me to do.

SALES COACH: I appreciate your telling me how you feel. What makes you think that's how we should work together? . . . If I thought telling you what to do would be as effective as helping you think this through yourself, I would.

Objections to the Obstacle

Some salespeople may not even acknowledge that there is an obstacle, or may disagree about how to remove it or what the solution should be. For example, one sales coach faced a salesperson who was emphatic: "When my contact says no, there is nothing I can do. It is impossible. I can't get to the director. I can't go over my customer's head."

Instead of telling the salesperson that she was giving up too easily and telling her how to uptier without disrupting a relationship with the current contact, the sales manager used questions: "I know it's important to preserve your relationships. Why do you think your contact isn't willing to . . .?" "How did you position the request to him?"

When you confront resistance, avoid two things: flight (don't give in) and fight (don't get defensive, attack). Instead, use the Objection Resolution Model:

- *Acknowledgment.* Show that you are listening and are interested in the salesperson's perceptions.

- *Probe.* Ask a question to further clarify, listen to the answer, and then most likely drill down further.

- *Position.* Share your perspective and include benefits to the salesperson to be more persuasive.

- *Check.* Ask a question to find out if you have agreement.

For example:

SALESPERSON: The relationships I have in place are so strong, they would tell me if there were additional needs within their area or in other areas of the company.

SALES COACH: I understand that you have strong relationships that you've worked hard to build. What makes you think that your customers will come to you with needs? . . . Who are the competitors who are calling on them? To what extent are you bringing ideas to your customers?

> *When you confront resistance, avoid two things: flight and fight.*

Questioning in selling is so important, and one of the halo benefits of *coaching by asking* is that you role-model effective selling and relationship skills.

Feedback is the language

of champion sales managers.

5

Developmental Sales Coaching—Feedback

In our management seminars, we frequently ask sales managers to think about a salesperson on their team who is overdue for feedback. Immediately, each sales manager can identify someone. We then ask how long the problem has been going on. They smile and squirm. Why? Often their answer is weeks or months. Many of the sales managers acknowledge that they *avoid* giving feedback. They explain that they don't feel comfortable doing so, and that they want to avoid confrontation. Or they don't want to damage the relationships or are not sure what to do.

When we ask sales managers to describe what good feedback sounds like, they easily come up with excellent guidelines. Nevertheless, it is challenging for them to put what they instinctively know into practice.

Feedback is the process of describing to a salesperson your perception of his behaviors or actions and the impact that those behaviors or actions are having on someone or something.

Feedback is *one* of the most important *parts* of the Developmental Sales Coaching process, but feedback by itself is *not* coaching. It is the *part of sales coaching where you share your perceptions with a salesperson.*

Whenever there is lots of open, balanced feedback going on in an organization, up and down and sideways, it is almost always a clear sign that the organization is in the Stretch Zone and that people are learning and changing. But organizations where feedback is a part of the culture remain the exception, not the rule. Too often feedback is met with rebuttal and rejection, rather than with openness.

The word *feedback* was introduced into the English language in the 1920s to describe the unpleasant screeching sound that was emitted when the feed (sounds that enter a microphone) went haywire. Soon psychologists and the medical profession borrowed the word and gave it its clinical connotation. Then the word found its way into the lexicon of business. By the 1980s, it wasn't uncommon to hear a comment such as, "Has anyone given Bob feedback on his voice mails (or you fill in the blank)?" Whether or not Bob ever got the feedback is another question.

In business today, unfortunately, many professionals think of feedback as confrontational. When they hear the word *feedback,* their ego goes up and their receptivity goes down. People can react negatively, both physically (heart pounding, dry throat) and mentally (fearful, nervous, defensive), expecting to hear about their shortcomings or face attack. Unfortunately, too often this is how they've experienced feedback.

It's not just salespeople who tense up at the thought of being recipients of feedback. As we've said, many sales managers are uncomfortable giving feedback, even when the feedback could make a significant difference to the success of a salesperson. Whether the reason is to avoid confrontation, not wanting to hurt a relationship, or the fear of demotivating or even losing a salesperson or having to deal with a salesperson who won't comply, many sales managers avoid it. Many go for days or months without giving *any* feedback. Some wait until a situation is at a crisis stage or they literally can't take it anymore.

As long as feedback is thought of as confrontational, there will be stress attached to it, and wanting to avoid it will be a natural response. In fact, effective feedback is far from confrontational—*it is a gift.* While giving feedback may not always be easy, your *intent* and *skills* can make giving even the most challenging feedback developmental and supportive and *not* confrontational. Our experience with thousands of sales professionals shows that once sales managers and salespeople experience balanced, *developmental* feedback, *they are hungry for more.* In fact, participant evaluations from our seminars and from our e-learning QuickSkills programs rank the intense feedback they get as the most valuable part of the learning.

What makes this even more impressive is that the seminar feedback is given by a trainer and peers in a group setting, which can make hearing feedback more challenging. When seminar participants are asked what reinforcement would be most valuable post-training, they ask for *more feedback.*

> *While giving feedback may not always be easy, your* intent *and* skills *can make giving even the most challenging feedback developmental and* supportive *and* not *confrontational.*

Your attitude toward feedback is the barometer for how your sales team feels about feedback. Your salespeople watch more than they listen, and the message you send about feedback will tell them how to respond to it and use it. Are you comfortable giving and getting feedback? Do you seek it out? Is the feedback you give only evaluative (to give a grade), or also developmental (to help someone improve)? What is your intent—to help them or to "get" them?

Evaluative and Developmental Feedback

There are two kinds of feedback, evaluative and developmental. Evaluative feedback assesses performance. Developmental feedback improves performance. Evaluative feedback involves a grade, and developmental feedback provides the support to improve that grade. Although evaluative feedback and developmental feedback are both essential and are linked, they are different. They are not merely two dialects. Look at them almost as two languages.

> *Your attitude toward feedback is the barometer for how your sales team feels about feedback.*

Evaluative Feedback

Evaluative feedback is what most salespeople think of when they hear the word *feedback*. Evaluative feedback is the language of the annual and quarterly performance review. It looks *back*. It represents yesterday, not tomorrow. If an Olympic athlete gets an 8.8, it does not make her better or worse. It is a score, a grade, an evaluation. Only what has happened before and what happens after that score impacts the performance.

Evaluative feedback is an essential part of sales management. It is based on the familiar model of grading found in schools: A through F, a quartile, a ranking of 1 to 5. It allows for comparisons—"You outperformed/underperformed"—and it is usually related to compensation, although ideally compensation is handled at a separate time.

During the performance review, your job is to give a rating—a *snapshot or picture of the past*—that captures your and your organization's perception of the salesperson being evaluated.

The primary goal of evaluative feedback is to make sure that the salesperson clearly understands, although she does not necessarily have to agree with, the rating/picture of the past. Evaluative feedback can be more limited or come from multiple sources, such as 360-degree feedback. Evaluative feedback is generally given once a year and is supported by a quarterly evaluation session. It is generally delivered by the sales manager. (Please see Chapter 10 for a discussion of performance reviews.)

Developmental Feedback

Developmental feedback is the feedback of coaching. It looks *forward* to what "we" (you and the salesperson) can do to improve performance and in the long run create a better picture (rating or grade) for the next evaluation period or future.

Developmental feedback is not limited to one or four times a year. *The time for Developmental Sales Coaching is always—daily in planned coaching sessions, in spontaneous coaching sessions, and in the corridor.* Developmental feedback answers the questions, "What can we do better to meet/exceed plan?" and "How can we improve . . . ?" While the responsibility for their improvement lies with salespeople, your role is to provide the forum where improvement can happen. Developmental feedback can come from peers, colleagues, and customers, although you are the primary source.

When one sales manager learned that there was a difference between evaluative and developmental feedback, he gave a sigh of relief. He said, "That's great. You mean I don't have to evaluate my salespeople every time I meet with them?"

Developmental feedback is a big part of Developmental Sales Coaching. It is *how you add value* by supporting salespeople in recognizing and removing obstacles. While both evaluative and developmental feedback are essential to sales management, developmental feedback is the type that leads to *improvement*. It is the type that encourages salespeople to stretch. Moreover, you are duty bound to give salespeople feedback when you have information that may be holding them back or stopping them from being as successful as they could be—or leading them to fail.

> *Developmental feedback is the type that leads to improvement.*

Developmental Feedback Guidelines

Let's look at practical feedback guidelines that you can use to increase your effectiveness and comfort level with making feedback a part of working with your salespeople every day.

Accurate

Check your facts. If you have any questions, do more research. Avoid assumptions; if you are missing any information, do your homework and/or ask the salesperson for his perspective before giving your feedback.

No Overload: One Focus—15 Minutes

It's almost impossible to improve several things at once. Salespeople can absorb just so much at one time. Avoid overwhelming them with too much feedback in one sitting. Effective feedback is incremental, and focusing on *one* priority at a time produces the *best results*. This also helps you keep coaching meetings to *15 minutes or less*. Identify a priority and deliver that message. Lesser points will only dilute the message and create confusion as to what to focus on. Cover lesser points later.

Even when you feel that there are numerous important priorities (the salesperson has a product knowledge deficit, can't close, and is poor at preparation), resist giving feedback on multiple things at once. Identify what is most pressing. Choose the thing that will have the greatest impact, and give feedback on that before moving on to the next priority.

> *Effective feedback is incremental, and focusing on one priority at a time produces the best results.*

Balanced

Provide feedback on both *strengths* and *areas for improvement* to create a *balanced picture*. No one is perfect in the absolute sense, and no one completely lacks strengths. When you give feedback, *start with strengths*—not just to be nice, although that does not hurt, but to set a positive tone and communicate that you are aware of the strengths. Moreover, salespeople can learn as much from their strengths as from their areas for improvement.

Even if salespeople say they want to hear only the negatives, provide positive feedback. If they don't hear positives, salespeople may easily feel that the "negative" feedback represents your total feelings about them. Presenting strengths is more than a formality and demands as much energy and attention as discussing areas for improvement.

One national sales manager described the one and only time she got feedback in the previous *three* years. She hated it. The reason: her manager gave her one positive piece of feedback, which she described as "throwing her a bone," before his tirade of negatives.

She is not alone in her feelings. One man—who approached me at the end of a negotiation speech I had given to about 200 people— explained why he hadn't raised his hand when I asked for two volunteers for a role play. He described an experience several years earlier when he had volunteered to be the salesperson in a role play in front of a group of about 100 people. He said, "That speaker tore me to shreds. When he gave me his book at the end of his speech, I threw it on the table. He had humiliated me!"

This salesperson then went on to tell how much he appreciated the balance of positive and negative feedback I had given to the role-play volunteers from our audience. He said, "It was constructive. It didn't come off as criticism. We learned how to improve—but it was in a helpful, balanced way."

I had in fact given direct and honest feedback on both strengths and areas for improvement. The feedback was well received for several reasons. First and foremost, I gave specific positive feedback first, before "areas for improvement," which I did not refer to as "weaknesses" or "negatives." And while I did tone down the areas for improvement *slightly*, since this was not a one-on-one situation but a large group setting in which one person had been singled out, before the role play, I discussed with the audience the importance of open feedback for *getting to the next level*. I stressed that there is not much progress in work or personal life from repeating the same things over and over. Finally, I approached the volunteer who was to get the feedback as "everyman," representing all of us.

By starting with positive feedback, you send the message early on that you feel that the salesperson is competent, or at least is doing some things right. You build a positive foundation that makes it easier for the salesperson to accept the areas for improvement. It also reduces any feelings of discomfort with feedback that you may have. But at the heart of giving positive feedback is your belief in your salespeople and that by working together, you and they can learn and grow.

By balancing strengths and areas for improvement, you gain the trust of your salespeople and keep things in perspective. It is your job to observe *both* the strengths and the areas for improvement.

If you really can't find any positives in a particular situation, don't make them up. A fundamental of coaching is to be honest. You might say, "Because I am so focused on X, let's discuss. . . ." The point is that this is the exception, and there should be many, many more times when the feedback you give is balanced and even leans to the positive. Acknowledging the positives creates a full picture.

> *It is your job to observe* both *the strengths and the areas for improvement.*

Here are some examples of balancing strengths and areas for improvement when giving feedback:

- "Beth, I know you are putting in long days and handling 'fires' around here every day. I appreciate the job you are doing covering for Bob. Still, I would like to talk with you about your prospecting effort. I have looked at the app, and I noticed that of the 12 calls, only 3 were with prospective customers. We discussed that our priority and focus at this time is *new* business and what it will take to fill your pipeline. How does what you're doing support those objectives?"

- "Joe, I know you were here long into the night on Thursday to finish the proposal, and the . . . deal has been taking a lot of your time. This may be hard for you to hear. Sarah said that there were several errors in the proposal you prepared, . . . got client feedback that those errors cost us the deal. She sent me a copy of the proposal, and I took a look at it . . . and in the cover letter. What are your thoughts on this?"

If you are uncomfortable giving feedback, you may water it down or avoid giving it. One way to help make you feel more comfortable is to start with strengths and then give areas for improvement to balance your message.

Specific

We've all heard the expression, "People hear what they want to hear." This is called "selective listening." Therefore, when giving feedback, it is essential that you be as *specific* as possible by citing *examples.* Examples help salespeople understand the message. If you were to give feedback on something general, such as a salesperson's "attitude," you would leave room for debate because attitude is subjective. But if you translate something as general as "attitude" into specific actions or inactions, your feedback will be concrete, objective, and more credible.

For example, you might get to the issue of bad attitude by saying, "I noticed that in the past three weeks, you have come late to our meetings, have not contributed to our discussion, and aren't making eye contact, and today you chose a seat outside the group. What's going on? What do you think those *behaviors* communicate?"

We experienced the power of specific, concrete examples with one of our trainers. No matter how much training, coaching, and observation time we gave to her, she could not catch on to the core parts of our programs. Worse yet, she did not realize that she was not catching on! When asked how she felt she was doing, she would say, "Great! I'm really coming along. I know all the modules, and I'm ready for assignments." We shared our feedback as well as feedback from other trainers who felt uncomfortable teaming with her, but she strongly disagreed. Her perception was that she *could* do the job and *would* do the job, and that was that. We knew that we could not assign her to our clients. Finally one day her manager walked out of the conference room and returned with the PowerPoint he had used with her in her most recent train-the-trainer session. He flipped through several screens—"This is what you covered, but this is what you were supposed to cover," and on and on for five pages. A look of utter surprise appeared on her face. In one day she resigned. It wasn't until she was given absolute, concrete examples—pages of them—that she was able to see the mismatch. Of course, the purpose of feedback is to help people grow, *correct* problems, and *succeed*, but it also can help individuals realize when it is time to make a change.

One sales manager was able to help a salesperson who was new to her team. The sales manager had gotten mixed reviews from customers. After a team call, she thought she knew why. Following a call and quickly before the next one, she asked for his perceptions and then gave him feedback: His product knowledge was good. And so were his questions and his tailoring of the product to the needs he uncovered. It was his presence that needed work—specifically, his body language and how he introduced himself (for example, things as basic as using his first name *and* his surname when he introduced himself, leveraging his industry and his background, and improving his posture during the meeting). The salesperson thanked her and said that his previous company was very casual. Five minutes of In-the-Action Coaching (see Chapter 7) had a dramatic impact on how he presented himself in the next call and how positively that customer responded to him.

Whether your feedback is based on your observations, data, or third-party input, use it to help your salespeople improve.

Impact

Once you give specific feedback and cite examples, go one step further—describe the *impact* of that behavior or action. Not only will this help make the message more objective and clear, it will reinforce the *need for change.* For example, "Joe, I know you were here long into the night on Thursday to finish the proposal to meet the short time frame. There were several errors in the proposal that caused concern to the customer, and *they are going with our competitor (impact—loss of the deal).*"

On Time

Give feedback as *close to the event* as possible. Delaying feedback usually causes the problem to fester and get worse. Timely feedback can help prevent a repetition of the same problem. Moreover, because the situation is fresh, the coaching is likely to have more impact. Timing also underscores the importance of the situation. Giving feedback "as you go" prevents things from bottling up and getting repeated. It also helps avoid surprises at performance review time, when it is too late.

Current

As much as possible, find current examples rather than relying on ancient history. The more specific and current the examples, the clearer the message. However, you can use past examples to show a pattern.

Open and Honest

Pulling punches usually does not help anyone. Your job is to say what others may not have the courage to say. The rule of thumb is that you can give feedback (in private) on anything a salesperson can correct that relates to her performance at work. For example, if a salesperson is short, growing taller is not a topic for coaching. But anything the salesperson can change that relates to her work is appropriate.

Some topics may be more uncomfortable to discuss, but salespeople have a right to know any information that you feel may be hindering their success. One salesperson recognized this when he said, "I'd be pretty upset if my boss, by withholding information from me, ultimately hurt my career." If you water down the message, the salesperson will miss the point. Being open and honest does not mean being brutal. You can be frank

> *Timely feedback can help prevent a repetition of the same problem.*

without being insensitive. You can say something like, "I know this may be heard to hear . . . ." Of course, if you have any doubt about an issue (for example, dress), check with your human resources group.

Being open and honest and receptive to feedback yourself will help your salespeople trust you. Salespeople fairly quickly form accurate judgments about who is "for" them and who is "against" them. Unless you are a good actor, you won't be able to fake or engender trust. When you have a positive attitude about feedback and are skilled in giving it, and if your intent is to help, your salespeople will see you as someone they can trust.

A salesperson's openness to feedback is usually proportionate to his level of trust. Trust is shaped by experience. It starts with you believing that your salespeople want to and can do a good job. As you coach salespeople, you show them that you are committed to and capable of helping them succeed.

Great managers are good coaches, not bad cops. Their message is, "I want to help," not, "I'm out to get you." They reward, help, and guide, not penalize, harass, and dictate. They separate development from evaluation.

Confidential

Provide feedback that is specific to salespeople privately in one-on-one coaching meetings. It's inappropriate to give developmental

feedback to salespeople in the presence of their peers or in any public forum. Group feedback is appropriate only if the feedback affects
the team and the team is ready for it. (Please see Chapter 8 on coaching the team.)

You can say almost anything to one of your salespeople one-on-
one behind a closed door. In one-on-one situations, even if you go
a little too far, an apology such as, "I'm
sorry, that was out of line," will almost
always be accepted. But if you embarrass
a salesperson in the presence of others—
if you cause her to lose face—you can
create a long-term enemy and cause irre-
versible damage to the relationship. Even
in private dialogues, choose your words
carefully because certain words can leave an indelible mark.

*Provide feedback
that is specific to
salespeople
privately in one-on-
one coaching
meetings.*

For example, an industry leader hired one of its retired senior
salespeople to provide sales training for its trainees. This "trainer"
abused his feedback rights. During the seminar, he gave harsh feedback to one of the participants who said that he would be "less than
honest" with the client in handling a sales problem. Certainly this
kind of thinking is unacceptable and demands correcting. Instead of
clearly defining the ethical standards of the firm and then suggesting
discussing this further one-on-one with the participant at the end of
the seminar, however, the senior salesperson/"trainer" attacked the
participant's values, ethics, and character as his associates watched in
silence—and in shock! The young man sat motionless as the tirade
went on *and on.* The only sign of the young man's reaction was the
quivering of his lower lip. Three weeks later, this hand-selected can-
didate (one of 60 out of 500 candidates) resigned from the program,
saying that he did not feel he could recover from this humiliation.

But the damage didn't end there. The impact lingered throughout much of the two-week-long training program. Fear was the

name of the game. The tragedy is that this seasoned salesperson/"trainer" had an opportunity to influence not only that trainee but 59 other young people on all of the values of the firm. But instead, because he lashed out in public, he was a force of destruction. He lacked any judgment or skill about giving feedback. The good news is that the firm's management took what they then called a "loose cannon" and asked me to coach him. He truly began to change. Although at first he was resistant to "babying" people with positive feedback and strongly tempering his so-called frankness (brutality), he eventually turned around so much that he began to use balanced and tempered feedback not only at work but at home and reported better relationships.

Everyone knows that a sales manager (in this case the trainer) has the authority to give strong feedback publicly. But when you have power, showing restraint in the presence of others is even more powerful. A perfect example of this brand of humility was exhibited by a judge in a nationally televised trial. The judge had been unflinching in his decision to hold the prosecutor in contempt if he did not apologize to the court, but the judge exceeded all expectations when, after receiving the prosecutor's apology, he apologized in return.

Developmental

Developmental Sales Coaching is proactive and consistent, not reactive and at the last minute. It is not "triage coaching," which is applied when things are out of control to try to change them radically in a short time frame. Triage coaching often shows up at the annual performance evaluation, where changes that should have been discussed during the previous 11 months are covered in one hour. Developmental Sales Coaching isn't touch and go. It is developmental and strategic. Triage coaching at best usually gets the valleys to the flat line (neutral performance), but it doesn't reach the peaks.

Developmental Sales Coaching is incremental and by working on *one* thing at a time over time it leads to faster results. It gives each priority the focus it needs to make a difference. It also helps keep the coaching meeting to 15 minutes or under. The power of incremental feedback is exponential.

Tone

Your job is to give feedback in such a way that the salespeople can hear it—and get it. When feedback is delivered in a confrontational, judgmental, or attacking manner, salespeople are less likely to be open to it. They are more likely to feel panic and resentment. By taking the evaluative element out of sales coaching, you help salespeople be more open to acknowledging their vulnerabilities and accepting your ideas. If you are angry when you are giving feedback, your anger, not the message, will be what you predominantly communicate.

> *The power of incremental feedback is exponential.*

Certainly you have the right and the obligation, as part of being open and honest, to express your concern about something, particularly if it is repeated, but if you are angry ("steaming"), that is *not* the time to give feedback. The anger will block both you and the salesperson from listening or solving the problem. First, calm down and delay giving feedback until a little later, when you can be calmer and more in control. When you deliver the feedback, be direct and clear about the severity of the situation in a way that encourages acceptance and change.

> *Your job is to give feedback in such a way that the salespeople can hear it and get it.*

Direct

Whenever possible, don't be a go-between for your salespeople when feedback from a third party is involved. This doesn't mean that you shouldn't support your people. However, if, for example, a salesperson complains about a team member, encourage the salesperson to give feedback to that person directly. While this may be met with resistance, you can coach the salesperson to help her take responsibility. A typical go-between conversation goes like this:

- Don't:

  SALESPERSON: Joe (an internal colleague) gave us lousy pricing again. We lost the deal. This is the second time this week. You have to help me with Joe. You've got to talk to him.

  SALES MANAGER (as go-between): What happened? . . . I'll talk to Joe. Don't worry. I'll take care of this.

- Do:

  SALESPERSON: Joe (internal colleague) gave us lousy pricing again. We lost the deal. This is the second time this week. You have to help me with Joe. You've got to talk to him.

  SALES COACH: That doesn't sound good. What happened? *Have you spoken to Joe?*

  SALESPERSON: It won't do any good. He won't listen to me. You know that.

  SALES COACH: Well, have you talked to him about this? *(repeat the question)*

  SALESPERSON: No. But it won't do any good. Maybe you can go to his boss.

SALES COACH: Well, before we go around him, what do you think about giving him feedback directly so that he understands how *you* feel and the *impact* he is having?

People at all levels in any organization often resist giving direct feedback to colleagues, especially if the culture hasn't supported doing so. But as mentioned earlier, your role is to help each person stretch and learn to remove both the current obstacle *and the next one.*

Of course, once the salesperson has given feedback directly to the colleague, if there are no results, then you can interview the colleague or elevate the discussion to the appropriate level.

If a salesperson simply will not or cannot give feedback to the person with whom he is having problems, you can suggest a three-way conversation in which you go *with* him, not *for* him. If the feedback involves giving feedback to a senior person, in most organizations it is your job to carry the message, not the salesperson's.

Receiving Feedback

Giving feedback is only half of the equation. Listening to feedback is the other half, and it can be challenging. There is a natural tendency for people to listen to what they don't agree with, not what they can learn from and use. Listening to feedback requires fighting the "self talk" that rejects what is being said with thoughts such as, "He doesn't understand." "But my reason for doing . . . was. . . ."

To get the most from feedback:

- Don't interrupt or explain.

- Ask questions to learn more.

- Take notes.

- Thank the giver.

■ Reflect on the feedback and use it to improve.

■ Ask for feedback from your manager, peers, and salespeople.

The "Feedback Conversation"

One sales manager who was excited about the idea of making feedback and Developmental Sales Coaching a way of life asked a question you also may be thinking about. When he asked, "Won't it seem odd to my salespeople if I all of a sudden start giving feedback and/or coaching?" his question was met with a lot of nods of agreement by his colleagues.

If your team is not accustomed to getting ongoing feedback and coaching, engage in a "feedback conversation" to prepare them. Tell them that you will be providing more feedback and coaching. To help get their buy-in, and in the spirit of "they talk first," ask them to help set the ground rules for giving and getting feedback. Letting them participate in developing the guidelines will help reduce any defensiveness they may be feeling. Discuss with them how you will work together to develop a coaching plan. (Please see the discussion of coaching plans in Chapter 6.)

In the "feedback conversation," discuss the responsibility of the giver of feedback to be frank and of the recipient to be open. Talk about the tendency of the recipient to become defensive and reject feedback and the detrimental impact that has on improvement. Invite them to give feedback to you.

Praise

A long while ago, a very talented young salesperson in our company came and asked in an almost pleading manner for more positive feedback. We were so busy growing that we didn't get around to praise very often. Within six months she resigned, and we learned a hard lesson. Her performance was excellent, and she was a pleasure to work with. She always took the initiative in asking for what she needed in order to do her best work—as evidenced by her request. Her departure was a loss. Most salespeople won't ask for praise the way she did. But without praise, salespeople can feel unappreciated, like a cog in a wheel rather than an important part of a team effort.

One kind of feedback that should be easy to give is praise. One would think that sales managers would seize every opportunity to do so. Yet the pressures of doing business every day and the lack of role models results in sales managers missing countless opportunities to show appreciation and celebrate successes. Giving praise is more than saying, "Good job." Of course positive quick comments are very good, but praise is so much more. Take a moment to ask questions such as, "How did you manage that?" Find ways to showcase accomplishments to the team and the organization. Many members of the new workforce are used to praise. They grew up on it. They require it. Part of being a great sales coach is taking the time to recognize good people and good work. Make praise a part of your coaching plans.

> *Without praise, salespeople can feel unappreciated, like a cog in a wheel rather than an important part of a team effort.*

As you praise a salesperson:

- Acknowledge the accomplishment in a genuine way. Describe the impact. Use examples and avoid exaggeration.

- Ask a question to create a dialogue so that the salesperson can share and savor the moment. Don't dilute the praise message by bringing up an area for improvement.

■ Thank the salesperson.

■ Find a way to showcase the salesperson's success. Recognize and reward that success.

■ Leverage the salesperson's ability to develop others.

To change behavior,

coach to a plan.

6

Developmental Sales Coaching—Focus and Discipline

Focus and discipline provide the management dimension of sales coaching.

Salespeople commit to carry out specific coaching action steps. Commitment is mutual. Your commitment comes in the form of your dedication and in setting clear objectives and the consistency and quality of your sales coaching (for example, noticing interim progress or issues, providing ongoing support and feedback) and your *follow-up*.

Knowing how often to coach, maximizing proactive and reactive coaching opportunities, allocating time among salespeople, balancing face-to-face and phone coaching, scheduling team calls and observations, and getting coaching for yourself demand planning.

Sales Coaching Plans

Sales Coaching Plans help turn intention into action. Certainly it is appropriate to seize spontaneous, quick sales coaching opportunities. However, as previously said, spontaneous coaching isn't enough. Planning is needed or sales coaching will remain the missing sales management discipline.

By developing Quarterly Sales Coaching Plans *with* your salespeople you gain their input and buy-in, you clarify expectations, and you create a coaching discipline. Keep the plans brief (one page) and simple, and use them to set sales coaching objectives and priorities and to measure the results of your coaching.

Allocating Time

80/20

As a sales manager, what percentage of your time do you dedicate to sales coaching? Is it enough?

Clearly, you are pulled in many directions. Day-to-day issues can fill the day—particularly if you are "doing" rather than coaching. Making a commitment to sales coaching often requires a significant reallocation of your time and a shifting of your priorities. The 80/20 rule proves true again: ideally, about 80 percent of your management time can be dedicated to sales coaching.

Factors such as the nature and complexity of your business, the skill level and tenure of your team members, and the team's experience in working together help determine how much time to spend with each salesperson. In general, the ideal number of direct reports on a sales team is six to eight salespeople per sales manager. And the ideal number of sales managers per regional manager is four to five. So time allocation must be thought through.

Quarterly Sales Coaching Plans for Salespeople

In the plan, include:

Salesperson: _____ Quarter: ____ Sales Coach: _____

Quarterly Objectives
- Quantitative Objectives Met _____ ❏ Yes ❏ No
- Quarterly Goal: _____
- Progress against Annual Goal: _____
- Qualitative Objectives
  - Priorities
  - Skill Enhancement

Coaching Schedule
- # of Proactive face-to-face sessions _____
- Dates/Times
- # of Remote sessions _____
- Dates/Times
- Observations _____
- # of Times to Praise _____

Post-Sales Coaching Summary for the Quarter
- Significant improvements
- Critical incidents

Sales Coaching Focus for Next Quarter

Sales Manager Quarterly Coaching Plans

Just as you develop a one-page Quarterly Coaching Plan for each salesperson, create one for yourself and include the following:

Past-Quarter Assessment	Yes	No
Did I coach to plan?	❏	❏
Did I achieve my goals?	❏	❏
Did I meet target?	❏	❏

Self-Coaching
- What did I do well as a sales coach?
- What will I do differently next quarter?

Coaching by My Manager
- # of coaching sessions with my manager _____
- Feedback from my sales members/team/colleagues

Coaching Focus for Next Quarter

(Please see the Model Quarterly Sales Coaching Plans at the end of this chapter.)

A rule of thumb is to allocate a minimum of three hours of one-on-one coaching each month for each salesperson. This can be face-to-face or by phone, depending on the situation. Ideally, in addition to this, observe each salesperson for a half day each month.

> *Making a commitment to sales coaching often requires a significant reallocation of your time and a shifting of your priorities.*

Of course, if you have a remote team—i.e., if travel is necessary to get together—you can plan a full day, for example, coaching in the morning and observing calls in the afternoon. With remote teams, the telephone can also be used effectively to coach. (Please see the discussion of remote coaching in Chapter 7.)

These are general guidelines to be adjusted based on circumstances. To help you think about how to allocate your time, start by grouping your sales team members in categories, for example, Red, Yellow, and Green—Underperformers, Midtier Performers, and Top Performers. Add to this a dimension for members who are new to your team or salespeople who are new to sales, and build in more face-to-face time with these new members early on to develop relationships with them.

Some guidelines for allocating time:

- *Top Performers.* At a minimum, one sales coaching meeting a month. Enlist their help to develop others on the team.

- *Midtier Performers.* Spend most of your time with this group to help them reach their potential.

- *Underperformers.* Many sales managers spend too much time with this group. This doesn't mean that you shouldn't spend time with them. In fact, quite the opposite is true—but with clear limits and objectives with specific time frames, and within that defined time, spend up to 40 percent of your time with underperformers. Our experience shows that you can probably save all but 5 or 6 percent. If you think about the impact of making this group productive—reducing turnover, helping them succeed, avoiding disruption to customers, not leaving territories unattended, not being short-staffed, and not having to recruit—it is much more than worth the effort.

One Focus/15 Minutes

Limiting the focus of each coaching meeting makes consistent and frequent sales coaching practical. Make sure your sales coaching meetings don't turn into marathons. When you focus on one thing at a time, you can lead most sales coaching sessions in 15 minutes or under. One-focus coaching not only makes consistent coaching practical, but achieves the best results most quickly. To respect everyone's time, start and stop on time.

Preparation and Follow-Up

Your level of preparation and the consistency of your follow-up are clear signals to your team about how serious you are about sales coaching as the strategy to develop them, achieve revenue, and grow relationships.

Preparing to Coach

Preparing to coach doesn't require a lot of time. Once you have established a coaching routine and have your one-page quarterly coaching plans, your preparation time gets shorter and shorter.

Depending on the focus of your coaching, your preparation can include researching the salesperson's progress against objectives, reviewing the coaching plan, or revisiting the agreement from the previous coaching session.

Before each sales coaching meeting, set one specific measurable *objective* to increase the likelihood that you will achieve the desired outcome. As you prepare your feedback, include *strengths* and

> *Preparing to coach doesn't require a lot of time.*

areas for improvement and recent examples. Think about the questions you will ask. Anticipate how you think the salesperson will react. If you are new to Developmental Sales Coaching, review the model.

The objective of the coaching session can be determined either by you or by the salesperson. To be meaningful, an objective should be measurable so that it describes a specific outcome and includes time frames for completion.

As you develop your objectives, think about them in positive terms—what you would like to see happen, not what you don't want to see. A negatively phrased objective will result in the salesperson understanding what not to do but not necessarily what to do.

One sales manager was very clear as he set his objective before a coaching session with one of his senior salespeople. The salesperson hadn't known that one of her major customers was issuing a big RFP. The sales manager's objective for the coaching was to help the salesperson develop strategies and a customer con-

> *Before each sales coaching meeting, set one specific measurable objective to increase the likelihood that you will achieve the desired outcome.*

tact plan to ensure that she not only would always be aware that an RFP was coming, but would be in a position to avert or influence the

RFP. He then prepared his questions, for example, "Erin, I know this caught us by surprise. Why do you think we weren't aware that . . . was issuing this RFP?"

Of course, *your* objective is one part of the picture. It is the starting point. But your chances of achieving it are greatly improved by understanding the salesperson's objective before trying to achieve yours. (Please see the Coaching Planner and Follow-Up at the end of this chapter.)

Debriefing the Coaching Session

Once the sales coaching session is over, debrief the session to *give yourself feedback*. At the end of a coaching session, you also have the option of asking the salesperson for feedback on the coaching—what was helpful and what he'd like more of/less of. (Please see the Sales Manager Postcoaching Debriefing at the end of this chapter.)

Follow-Up

To expect is one thing. To inspect is another. You show that you are committed to sales coaching by consistently following-up flawlessly. Your salespeople will figure out very quickly whether or not you follow through. When your salespeople know that you are aware of what's going on and that you don't let things slide, when your comments show that you are on top of things, they will be very attentive to what they've committed to during coaching sessions. If you don't follow up, they'll read that as your not feeling that the agreement was important. If it's not important to you, it won't be important to them.

You are the role model. Everything you do serves as an example. If you want salespeople to sell by asking, coach by asking. If you want them to be responsive, be responsive. If you want them to follow up, follow up. Set clear specific, action steps with a time frame at the end of each coaching session and tickle them in your calendar.

> *You are the role model.*

The objective of follow-up is to answer two questions, "Did the salesperson accomplish . . . ?" and "Where do we go from here?" Development is a journey, and it is incremental—it is about accomplishing one priority and moving on to the next. As one sales coach phrased it, "That was round one. Now let's go to round two."

> *Development is a journey, and it is incremental.*

In the perfect world, salespeople would come to you for follow-up. In the real world, it is your job.

Quarterly Developmental Sales Coaching Plan

Please complete this kind of information one time per quarter for each salesperson on your team.

Salesperson: _____   Sales Coach: _____

Salesperson's Qualitative Quarterly Objectives (nonrevenue) (for example: mix of products/product knowledge)

Skill Enhancement for Quarter

- Two key strengths to build on:
  1.
  2.
- Two priority areas for improvement:
  1.
  2.

Comments:

Progress against Revenue Goal

Quarterly Goal: $ _____

- Is the salesperson on target to meet quarterly goal? ❑ Yes ❑ No
- Met quarterly goal? ❑ Yes ❑ No

Gap:

_____

Action Plan:

_____

Coaching Schedule

- # of proactive scheduled face-to-face sessions per quarter: _____
  - Dates/Times:
- # of proactive remote coaching sessions per quarter: _____
  - Dates/Times:
- # of Observations: _____
- # of times to give praise: _____
  - Dates/Times:

Total Coaching Time Commitment Anticipated: _____ hours

Coach Observations

- What significant change/improvement did you see?

- Action Steps Agreed to:

Focus for Next Quarter:

Sales Manager's Quarterly Coaching Action Plans

Please complete this page once per quarter to assess your own strengths and areas for improvement as a coach to develop a coaching action plan for yourself.

Sales Coach: _____   Quarter: _____

Post-Quarter Self-Assessment
■ Did I coach to plan?   ❑ Yes   ❑ No
■ Did I achieve my coaching goals?   ❑ Yes   ❑ No
■ Did my team make target?   ❑ Yes   ❑ No

Self-Coaching
■ What did I do well as a sales coach?
■ What will I do differently next quarter?

Coaching by My Manager
■ # of coaching sessions by my manager _____
■ Feedback from my sales members/team/colleagues

Coaching Focus for Next Quarter
■ Two key strengths to build on:
   1.
   2.
■ Two priority areas for improvement:
   1.
   2.
Comments:

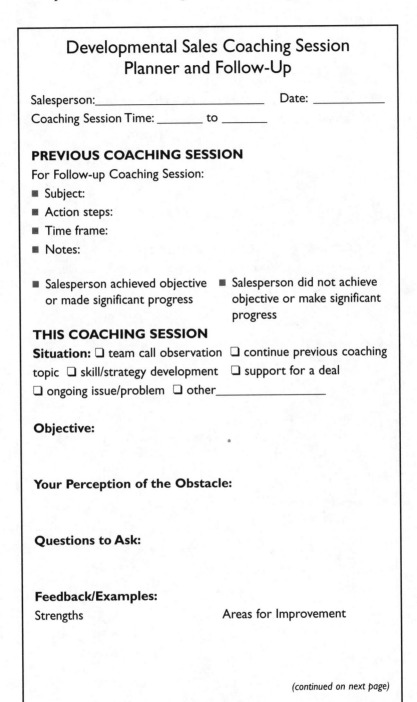

Developmental Sales Coaching Session Planner and Follow-Up

Salesperson:_____ Date: _____

Coaching Session Time: _____ to _____

PREVIOUS COACHING SESSION

For Follow-up Coaching Session:

- Subject:
- Action steps:
- Time frame:
- Notes:

- Salesperson achieved objective or made significant progress
- Salesperson did not achieve objective or make significant progress

THIS COACHING SESSION

Situation: ❑ team call observation ❑ continue previous coaching topic ❑ skill/strategy development ❑ support for a deal ❑ ongoing issue/problem ❑ other_____

Objective:

Your Perception of the Obstacle:

Questions to Ask:

Feedback/Examples:

Strengths   Areas for Improvement

(continued on next page)

Developmental Sales Coaching Session Planner and Follow-Up (continued)

Plan to Build Rapport and Strengthen Relationship: **Anticipated Objections:**

Action Step/Time Frame: **Support You Will Provide:**

POST-COACHING SESSION ANALYSIS

Focus of Coaching Session: ❑ As Planned   ❑ Varied from Plan—if so, describe: _____

- Progress made:
- Remaining issue (if appropriate):
- Action steps committed to/time frame:

Your Perceptions of Salesperson's	Excellent	Very Good	Good	Not Good
■ Responsiveness to coaching:	❑	❑	❑	❑
■ Insights into his/her own performance:	❑	❑	❑	❑
■ Assessment of progress being made in response to coaching:	❑	❑	❑	❑

Sales Manager's Postcoaching Debrief

	Yes	No
■ **Was I prepared?**		
– Did I set a measurable objective?	❑	❑
■ **Connect**		
– Did I build the relationship?	❑	❑
■ **Compare**		
– Did I ask rather than tell?	❑	❑
– Did I ask for the salesperson's perceptions before giving mine?	❑	❑
– Did I drill down to help the salesperson analyze/identify other possibilities?	❑	❑
– Did I share my perceptions?	❑	❑
– Did I check for agreement that a gap exists?	❑	❑
■ **Construct**		
– Did I ask the salesperson to identify the obstacle?	❑	❑
– Did I ask for the salesperson's ideas for how to remove the obstacle before giving my ideas?	❑	❑
– Did we practice?	❑	❑
– Did we agree on a plan of action?	❑	❑
■ **Commit**		
– Did I get buy-in on the agreement/next steps?	❑	❑
– Did I set clear next steps/time frame?	❑	❑
– Did I express my commitment?	❑	❑
– Did I encourage?	❑	❑

Great sales coaching can

overcome great distance.

7

Developmental Sales Coaching—Remote, Team, and In-the-Action Coaching

Organizations with remote sales forces often struggle to find ways to remove the feelings of isolation and detachment that can be common by-products of being out of touch. Without a strong support system, the best an organization can hope for is a group of independent salespeople with no real attachment.

Remote coaching is a strategy for developing salespeople and sales teams over long distances, across geographies, time zones, and cultures. Factors such as global teams, the trend toward home offices, and the cost of travel have increased the amount of remote coaching taking place today.

The big challenge for sales managers in remote coaching is the lack of face-to-face observation and personal contact. Salespeople face challenges too. They lack examples, miss role modeling, feel disconnected, and may not get the inspiration they need.

In a remote management environment, coaching is your primary tool for connecting with and developing your salespeople. Technology certainly has made connecting easier. However, technology alone can't compensate for a lack of face-to-face contact. Therefore, with remote salespeople it is essential to find ways to personally build relationships and work together physically when possible before relying on remote contact.

The Developmental Sales Coaching Model is effective in face-to-face and remote coaching situations. However, because of the lack of face-to-face contact that gives you qualitative data, there are four essentials that must be in place to make remote coaching work:

- *Performance metrics.* It is essential that you set clear, measurable objectives and know where the salesperson is against those objectives. After building rapport as you begin a remote coaching session, use the metrics as the starting point for looking at how the salesperson is doing. Although from your dashboard or other source of data, you will usually know where the salesperson stands against his objectives, ask for his perceptions first. By asking for his perceptions first, you will learn a lot. Some salespeople will have an accurate picture of their performance. For salespeople whose perceptions are different from yours and who are not facing the facts, your role is to help create awareness and correct the misperception so you can focus on strategies and close performance gaps. Because you usually won't have as much qualitative data available as when there is more face-to-face contact, begin at least one-half of your remote coaching sessions with a quick review of the salesperson's metrics against performance, but be careful not to let the session slip into an evaluative session. Keep the focus on what you can do to improve performance and build on strengths.

■ *Clear principles and parameters.* Remote salespeople require a tighter structure with clearly defined objectives and boundaries. They also need a few strong principles that are continuously reinforced, such as company values ("go crazy for customers" or "customers first" or "all e-mails are responded to within 24 hours"), and clear, specific parameters on their level of authority. It's also important to work with them to determine how corporate headquarters and you can add value and support them.

■ *Coaching process.* Salespeople need to be engaged during phone coaching calls. The Developmental Coaching Model allows for that, but you also must make two modifications when you are coaching remotely: start with metrics, and specifically include relationship building in the agenda. While it is not necessary to begin every remote coaching meeting with metrics, it is important that you discuss progress against objectives at least once each

> *Remote salespeople require a tighter structure with clearly defined objectives and boundaries.*

month. For example, as you begin Step 2, Compare Perceptions, consider saying, "Let's begin by looking at where you are against your objectives."

■ *Relationship focus.* By making the time to focus on the relationship, you can help put the qualitative element back in. Get to know your salespeople personally to establish a foundation of trust. With salespeople who are new to your team do all you can to explicitly work on the relationship in each coaching meeting. Because salespeople are remote, it is important, especially early in the relationship, to spend time face-to-face with them whenever possible.

The majority of your remote coaching is most likely to be by telephone. Telephone, voice mail, e-mail, chat, conference calls, Webinars, podcasts, text messaging, and video conferencing are all tools that you can use to work with your remote salespeople to keep them connected, plugged in, and "on."

Today some organizations are using high-definition, high-audio teleconferencing systems that are designed to duplicate a live face-to-face meeting experience. However, while technology such as this is very powerful, it cannot replace your first building an individual relationship with each salesperson.

Telephone

For remote coaching when face-to-face isn't possible, the telephone remains the most "warm," personal tool for one-on-one coaching. The telephone has many advantages, but it also has its share of drawbacks as a coaching tool. On the positive side, it allows for immediacy and convenience for reaching out. It allows for dialogue back and forth. It can even offer some distance, both physical and mental, which at times can be a good thing. Because it is immediate, interactive, and voice-to-voice, the telephone is the medium that is closest to face-to-face. It is also easier to take notes.

As for drawbacks, it's harder to establish and maintain rapport by phone. Everything can be magnified over the phone or be misinterpreted. Therefore, treat salespeople graciously, maintain a good tone, be careful with your wording, and listen more carefully. Prepare a written agenda for each call so that you don't forget items. The worst situation in phone coaching is one in which sales managers don't call unless there is a problem or don't return calls or encourage them from salespeople. When your salespeople call or e-mail, respond ASAP and *always* at a maximum within 24 hours.

To help you maximize your ability to coach by phone:

■ *Replicate face-to-face.* As much as possible, make it feel as if you are sitting down together. Because you have less face-to-face contact, make a specific point of taking a few minutes for personal rapport. Avoid interruptions and distractions. Without the benefit of body language to help you read the situation, it is especially important that you keep your focus on the salesperson and listen carefully for tone, intonation, pauses. . . .

■ *Be prepared/create your agenda.* For each call, create a written agenda of the topics you want to cover in the call. Set a coaching appointment for your proactive sales coaching sessions. Because the team is remote, you will probably set 30- to 60-minute coaching sessions in addition to your 15-minute sessions, and your face-to-face visits will likely cover one full day.

As for how to divide your coaching time among metrics, coaching, and relationship, spend about 5 percent on metrics (How are you doing against objectives?), and remember *they talk first.* Spend at least 80 percent of your time coaching (identify the gaps, obstacles, solution, practice, encouragement), and spend at least 5 percent building the relationship. (This is more than rapport building, which of course is still important. Explicitly talk about the relationship. Ask questions such as, "What can I be doing more of or less of to support you?") You will probably want to cover some other items when you have connected with salespeople. Complete the coaching agenda *before* discussing any administrative matters or updating. Spend 5 to 10% of the time on these agenda items.

To maximize each telephone call, keep your agenda in front of you to help ensure that you don't forget to cover anything. If there are documents that you and the salesperson will need during the coaching session, e-mail these materials in advance.

Ask salespeople to provide you with any materials you need
from them.

■ *Keep appointments.* Unless there is a very compelling reason,
don't cancel and don't be late. Respect the salesperson's schedule and start and stop on time. If you are calling without an
appointment, ask the salesperson if it's a good time to talk.

■ *Use multiple modes of communication* (phone, voice mail, text,
e-mail, chat).

Ideally, limit voice mail, text, and e-mail primarily to communicating positive messages, planning logistics, saying thank you, or
wishing the salesperson good luck on an upcoming call. One company uses real-time data from its dashboard to e-mail a message of
congratulations to the salesperson "as soon as the deal hits."

Voice Mail, E-mail, . . .

If you must "coach" by voice mail, e-mail, text . . . and leave a message about strengths *and* areas for improvement, take the time to edit
your messages for content and tone. Double-check your tone before
you hit the send key. Whenever possible, if the coaching topic is very
personal or very serious, opt for face-to-face. If it is not possible to
meet personally, use the phone if at all possible and always make it
clear that you'd prefer to be having the discussion in person.

When it is necessary to include areas for improvement, qualify
your message. It is likely that you don't have all the facts or perceptions. For example, say, "I'd rather be talking live and I don't have
your perspective. Based on my knowledge that . . ., I want you to
know. . . ." Pose a few questions. As you give feedback, give both the
strengths and the areas for improvement. End each message with an
action step and information on how and when the salesperson can

reach you. If it is essential to leave a critical/constructive message, especially if your voice mail system doesn't offer a "check your mes-sage" feature that allows you to edit, pre-pare what you will say. As you are leaving the message, if you have second thoughts about your message, hang up and start over. If you are upset, don't leave a voice mail message; send an e-mail or a text message. Wait until you calm down. One frustrated sales manager described how his senior uses voice mail as a "one-way assertion tool."

Limit voice mail, text, and e-mail primarily to communicating positive messages, planning logistics, saying thank you, or wishing the salesperson good luck on an upcoming call.

Be sure your message helps, not hurts, the situation. *When in doubt, don't.* Like any one-way mode of com-munication, voice mail and e-mail deprive salespeople of the opportunity to respond to you immedi-ately. If they can't tell their side of the story, they can become frus-trated and upset unnecessarily. Voice mail coaching also requires extra judgment and sensitivity. Phrase what you say carefully. Keep in mind that someone else may hear your message other than the salesperson for whom you are leaving the message. The salesper-son at that point can't respond to you—and may have had a bad day. Just imagine one of your salespeople picking up a negative message as she returns from an 11:00 p.m. delayed flight after a long day!

One voice mail message pushed a senior salesperson to resign. She received the message at the end of a long day following a diffi-cult team call with her manager, a specialist, and a junior team mem-ber. She let the specialist present the recommendations. Her strategy was to give the specialist a chance to build his credibility. Later that day, her sales manager left a stinging message that she picked up at

9:30 p.m. when she returned to her home. "Jean, I was very disappointed in your performance at the meeting. You sat there while Bob did all the talking. You should have had a stronger role. I'm disappointed and upset about your judgment!" For her it was the straw that broke the camel's back. This is a perfect example of how not to "coach." A different voice mail message could have strengthened the relationship—"Jean, hope your flight home was on time. Please give me a call. I'd like to debrief the call and talk about roles." Another sales manager used e-mail to help save a deal. He disagreed with a strategy that the salesperson was about to implement, and in his e-mail, he asked three questions, made one suggestion, and wished the salesperson luck.

As for using chat for coaching, the benefit is the immediacy of feedback. However, the drawback is the speed at which the dialogue can move. Remember to maintain a collaborative and supportive tone, ask questions, and give balanced feedback.

While there are pitfalls, with judgment and skill, phone, voice mail, e-mail, text, chat . . . can be effective coaching mediums for improving performance and building the relationship.

Remote Coaching Essentials

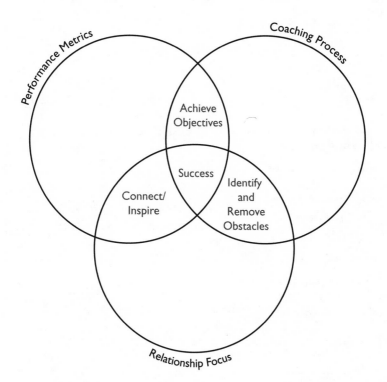

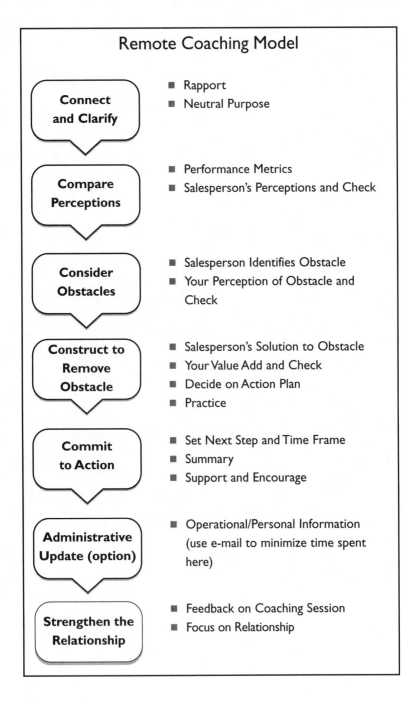

Remote Coaching Model

Connect and Clarify
- Rapport
- Neutral Purpose

Compare Perceptions
- Performance Metrics
- Salesperson's Perceptions and Check

Consider Obstacles
- Salesperson Identifies Obstacle
- Your Perception of Obstacle and Check

Construct to Remove Obstacle
- Salesperson's Solution to Obstacle
- Your Value Add and Check
- Decide on Action Plan
- Practice

Commit to Action
- Set Next Step and Time Frame
- Summary
- Support and Encourage

Administrative Update (option)
- Operational/Personal Information (use e-mail to minimize time spent here)

Strengthen the Relationship
- Feedback on Coaching Session
- Focus on Relationship

Team Call Coaching

Ideally, you will be out in the field with your salespeople a minimum of a half-day each month. Team calling gives you the opportunity to observe salespeople in action. It provides an ideal forum for pre- and postcall coaching. In most sales calls, your role is that of observer (although from the customer's perspective, it usually is to show management commitment to the relationship).

Your Role

Unless the team call has been arranged "senior to senior," your role is to *support* your salespeople. But customers and salespeople may defer to you because of your level. Therefore, it's important to make sure that the salespeople, not you, lead the call and that you aren't drawn into taking over the call. Even when customers direct questions to you, most of the time you can tactfully "turn them over." For example, if a customer directs a question to you (unless it is an executive-level question, such as asking you about your organization's commitment to the customer's industry), make a brief comment and redirect the question to the salesperson. You might say, "Bill, that's a great question. I feel that this is one of our strengths. We lead the charts in. . . . Janet has recently . . . with one of her customers, and she can describe how that worked with . . . and the results."

Customers will observe how you work with your salespeople. One salesperson described negative feedback he got from a customer who chose another provider because his sales manager not only dominated the call but spoke to him in a demeaning way and commanded, "Write that down so *you'll* remember to do it." The customer lost confidence in the salesperson's ability to lead the deal because he

Your role is to support your salespeople.

hadn't established his credibility during the call. Moreover, the customer was offended by the sales manager's behavior. Another salesperson complained that his sales manager "hogs" the calls.

Preparation

Preparing before the sales call gives you the chance to assess the salesperson's preparation, make adjustments to increase the effectiveness of the call, and agree on the area of development to focus on in the post-call debrief. Some sales managers and salespeople "wing it," or limit their preparation to discussing the technical aspects of the call or taking a minute or two before going into the call. Your expectations about preparation will set the standard for most of your salespeople. As you prepare, discuss more than the technical aspects of the call. Cover the strategy, skills, the agenda, roles, and call objective.

To help your salespeople prepare fully not only for calls with you but for all of their calls, ask them for their ideas and share with them your expectations for preparation.

At a minimum, salespeople must do the following to brief you for the call.

Provide background on the customer. The Web, SFA, and CRM have made doing homework and sharing information faster and easier then ever before. As you get briefed for the call, the salespeople should discuss with you the company's strategy, needs, status of the relationship, the call objective, an overview of what they plan to present, and any outstanding items. Ideally, they should give you a one-page summary. Ask salespeople if they have visited the customer's Web site and what insight they got. Check that the call objective is measurable and has a time frame.

Discuss the questions that they plan to ask, the objections that they anticipate hearing, and their desired action steps. It is very important to define roles and set the post-call development focus, such as probing to identify needs, cross-selling, value justification, or closing the deal. It is also helpful to ask the salesperson what she wants to focus on and gain agreement to debrief the call.

After your team call with your salesperson, take advantage of the immediacy and freshness of the call when the salesperson's and your perceptions are sharp and debrief the call. After you've debriefed the call a few times, you can do so very quickly. It becomes second nature and can be done in shorthand.

In-the-Action Coaching

While planned, proactive coaching is essential, spontaneous coaching opportunities arise often. Maximize every opportunity to coach. If you observe a salesperson not exhibiting the desired behavior, take a moment to ask her about the behavior you observed, give your feedback, and check for agreement. If a salesperson comes to you with a quick question or problem, rather than give the answer and encourage dependency, ask first, "What do you think?" or "What's the problem?" and then, "What's the obstacle?" and "What do you suggest doing?" before your give your perspective.

> *Maximize every opportunity to coach.*

You know it's a team when

salespeople coach each other.

8

Developmental Sales Coaching—Sales Meetings and Coaching Your Team

There are two ways to coach your salespeople—one-on-one and as a team. Up to this point, we have focused on one-on-one sales coaching. As powerful as one-on-one coaching sessions are, there is one thing they can't do: they can't help you build your team. To build a team, the team must be together.

Sales meetings are the perfect setting for coaching your salespeople as a team and encouraging them to coach one another. You need your salespeople to function as a team to build a commitment to the common goal that exceeds their own interests and to collaborate when jobs are interrelated.

As powerful as one-on-one coaching sessions are, they can't help you build your team.

As powerful as sales meetings can be, too often the potential for team synergy is lost. Rather than leveraging the opportunity of being together and sharing ideas and strategies, developing skills, and gaining commitment to the common goal, meeting time frequently is used to review data and focus on operational and administrative detail that could be covered in e-mails. Moreover, often there is a lack of participation and sharing of ideas.

Attitudes toward Sales Meetings

It's not uncommon to hear sales managers and salespeople alike complain that sales meetings waste their time. One company, in an effort to eliminate "meetingitis," created chair-free conference rooms designed to keep meetings short.

By managing both the content (what is on the agenda) and the process of the meeting (how you lead the meeting), you can turn sales meetings into a forum that salespeople look forward to for learning and support. The skills and process that you use in one-on-one coaching are a good base for leading sales meetings. However, just as it takes an additional set of skills to sell to a group compared to selling to one customer at a time, additional skills are needed to lead sales meetings to maximize the synergy that is only possible when the team is together.

The dynamics and challenges of working with a group of salespeople rather than one-on-one are different. For example, a comment that can be a toss-away in a one-on-one sales coaching situation can feel devastating to a salesperson in the presence of his peers. Leading a sales meeting demands that you draw on group sales presentation, team building, and meeting skills.

Leading Sales Meetings

Let's look at strategies, tactics, and skills for leading developmental, interactive sales meetings where team building happens. It takes a few principles and tools. One sales manager reported that he used his newfound sales meeting skills during a meeting of his condo association and was elected its new president!

Preparation

Before each meeting, set your objectives so that you are clear about what you want to accomplish. Because you will be working with a group, prepare a *written agenda* that bullets the points to be covered. Decide on the process you will use to cover each agenda item—for example, discussion, presentation, team activity, brainstorming, or reports by participants . . . and prepare the materials you will need. (Please see the Sales Meeting Agenda Planner at the end of this chapter.)

The Agenda

A written agenda is the most important tool you have for *controlling* your sales meetings. A sales meeting agenda should be simple and brief. Point by point, it lists on one sheet of paper or on a screen the topics for the meeting. It is not a bunch of scribbles on a scrap of paper that you hold during the meeting. It is important that you share this with your team members. Determine how much to include in an agenda based on the length of the meeting (i.e., 30 to 40 minutes) and the complexity of the topics to be covered.

If nothing else, your agenda will make the *purpose* of the meeting clear to participants and put the "I don't know why I'm here" complaint to rest. The agenda ensures that you get clarity on the purpose of the meeting, but it does not guarantee buy-in. An excellent way to foster *buy-in* is to give salespeople an opportunity to contribute to the agenda. A simple way to get their input is to ask at the end of every sales meeting for their ideas and suggestions for the next meeting. Simply ask, "We'll be meeting again on . . . (date). What priorities do you think we should address at that meeting?" You can also invite team members to add agenda items up to several days before the meeting.

To keep expectations clear, let participants know that you want and will use their ideas, but that the priorities for the agenda will be set by you. For example, you might delay a topic suggested by a salesperson or deal with it one-on-one or in a subgroup to accommodate other priorities. But if topics that are important to the sales force *never* make it to the agenda, it may be a sign that you need to rethink your priorities.

As a rule of thumb, salespeople should contribute about 30 percent of the agenda. When their ideas are on the agenda, they usually are on board too.

To make sure that the participants are clear about the objectives of the meeting, go over the agenda and ask for feedback. Here are some ideas for leveraging your agendas during sales meetings.

- *Build rapport.* Before distributing the agenda, build brief rapport. Allow for a comfortable setting and if possible include some refreshments.

> *Salespeople should contribute about 30 percent of the agenda.*

- *Distribute the agenda.* You may wish to distribute the agenda in advance, but this may not really be necessary.

- *Tour the agenda.* Once you have distributed the agenda, quickly "tour" the topics with a quick review. Don't expound on any points yet. The goal of the tour is to *headline* each topic so that salespeople have an overview of what needs to be accomplished.

- *Check the agenda.* Once you've completed the tour, check for agreement by asking, "What questions do you have about the agenda?" This check gives salespeople a chance to voice concerns or get clarification. Someone may ask, "Why are we covering X when we need to do Y?" When this happens, you have several choices. You can add the point to the agenda, but if you do, be careful not to lose track of the priority items on the agenda. If the agenda was jointly set, the salespeople have had the opportunity to add to it. You can table the new topic for another meeting or set a time to deal with the topic outside the meeting so that you can keep to the agenda.

■ *Guard the agenda.* Your role during a sales meeting is to be the *guardian of the agenda.* If someone takes the discussion off track onto a tangent, use the agenda to help the group stay focused. Like a goalie in ice hockey, your job is to keep an eye on the topic being discussed and *not* let other topics slip in and derail the discussion. A comment like, "Tom, that's an important point. We are talking about . . . and we need to complete [objective]. So can we hold that until . . . ? Let's go back to. . . . We can get to that point (the next agenda, possibly at the end of this meeting if there is time, or at another appropriate time)."

Only for a very compelling reason should you divert the meeting from its original objectives. You could say, "Let's start with the first topic. Since we have three topics to cover, and this is a big one, let's plan on spending about 10 minutes on it."

Only by guarding the agenda can you make headway. Think in terms of the objective for each agenda item. For example, if "offsetting . . . competitor" is an agenda item, the objective could be "To have Chris present his report on . . . competitor and have the team develop two strategies for positioning and winning against that competitor."

■ *Use the agenda to lead the meeting.* Leading the sales meeting is your job—at least initially. Open the meeting with rapport; tour the agenda; manage the agenda; say hello and good-bye to every agenda item. The hello identifies the topic; after you have covered the agenda item, decided on an action, and checked for questions, say good-bye to it with a comment such as, "OK, let's move on to. . . ."

Make Decisions

Before you move from one agenda item to the next, ask, "What action can we take here?" or "What have we decided to do about . . . ?" The action can be an assignment such as, "Jerry will look into . . . and report on . . ." or a decision such as, "We will increase . . . by . . . percent by. . . ."

I learned the value of taking action many years ago when I was a principal of a New York City high school. At each staff meeting over a period of *two or three months*, we discussed again and again the challenge of student lateness. Finally, at one meeting, a teacher said, "We've discussed this dozens of times. Let's either make some decision or not talk about it anymore." Her call to action caused everyone to sit up. We broke into three teams, and each one presented a recommendation. We selected one: stop serving breakfast (rolls and milk) at 8:55 a.m. Our lateness problem improved by 80 percent the first week. More significant than the fact that we came up with an effective solution, we made a pact to have a bent toward action for every agenda item. If the ideas we came up with didn't work, we tried something else. Talk turned into action steps.

Once the decision or action is set, be sure to *check*—"Before we move on, are there any questions? Let's summarize what has been decided."

Decision Minutes

Keep track of the decisions made, who is accountable for each decision, and the time frames. Decision Minutes are not the ordinary (tedious) "minutes" of a meeting that give a blow-by-blow account of everything anyone said or did. Decision Minutes summarize only decisions (action steps) committed to by the group or by a specific person. They clearly identify three things: who is accountable, what the task is, and the time frame for completion. Decision Minutes become the "to do" bible for *your follow-up* and for the *team members accountable.* They can usually be recorded on one page. (Please see the Decision Minutes at the end of this chapter.)

To start the process, you can volunteer to record the decisions for the *first* meeting. But to help establish shared responsibility for the sales meetings, after that ask for volunteers and rotate the responsibility.

Decision Minutes describe the output of the agenda. They help combat the feeling that nothing gets accomplished in meetings. In fact, usually the decision is to accomplish things outside the meeting, but the ball is put in motion. For example, if 10 minutes of the meeting is spent understanding the target market, customer needs, and the pitch for a new product, the action step could be to have each salesperson identify and call on five prospects for the product to sell it and bring feedback to the specialist within the next three weeks.

Whoever records Decision Minutes should read them and check for agreement. Prompt this by saying, "Let's listen to what was recorded." to make sure everyone is in agreement.

Having each decision in *writing* and backed by a *commitment to the group* by the salesperson who is accountable *increases group ownership* and *personal responsibility.* Of course, deciding on an action step and actually having it implemented are two different things. Decision Minutes are a great tool to *help* get things done, but they do not guarantee it. Your follow-up does.

Follow-up is your role after the sales meeting. That's why your name should stay out of the accountability column of the minutes. Don't fall into the trap of delegating to yourself. By keeping your name out of the accountability column, you will have time to follow up and provide support.

Decision Minutes should be a part of every sales meeting—if there are no decisions or next steps, it's probably a sign that not much was accomplished.

Group Participation

One of the goals for your sales meetings should be to encourage participation by all team members. In leading sales meetings, your job is to *interact*, not act, and rather than be on stage, be *in sync*. Many sales managers, because they have not had training in how to lead a meeting and have not had role models to show them how to do it, will tell rather than *team*.

> *Don't fall into the trap of delegating to yourself.*

Just as questioning is at the heart of one-on-one coaching, questions are the way to create interaction and generate energy during sales meetings. Initially, you will lead sales meetings, but with team meeting skills, you can help the group become more responsible for the quality and productivity of the meetings and share the responsibility among the team members.

Meetings by Questioning

Use your questioning skills to engage your salespeople and help make them responsible for the quality of the meetings.

- *Ask open-ended questions.* Questions that begin with words like *what, why,* and *how* help salespeople express and think through their ideas. For example, in discussing a prospecting phone blitz, instead of telling everyone how to handle gatekeepers, ask, "What are some things you do to get past and/or win over the gatekeepers?" Other examples are: "*What* has been your experience in calling customers to discuss . . . ?" "*How* did you determine whether . . . qualifies . . . ?" By avoiding closed-ended/ yes-or-no questions that begin with words like *do* and *are*, you encourage dialogue.

■ *Volley questions.* Salespeople are most likely to direct their questions, answers, and ideas to you. Channel their comments back to your team. Rather than being the "expert," encourage the sharing of ideas among the team. For example, you can say, "I am glad you brought that up. That objection can be tough. How are some of you dealing with it?" And when someone makes a point, ask the group members what they think rather than immediately giving your view or adding on ideas. You will encourage participation by holding off on giving your feedback and letting others give their ideas first. Then you can amplify or add to what others have said with comments such as, "That's an important perspective. I also think . . ." or, "John's idea is. . . . You can also. . . ."

■ *Elicit many views.* After one salesperson answers a question, don't stop there. Other salespeople have ideas too. By asking others for their views as well—"What about someone else? What have others of you found?"—you will stimulate a productive dialogue.

■ *Ask why.* Expand the discussion by asking, "Why is that?"

■ *Refrain from immediate judgment.* One of the worst things you can do is ask for input and immediately reject what a salesperson says. If you think that what is said is off the mark, you have several options:
  - Ask for the salesperson's thinking to more fully understand his point of view.
  - Get input from others: "What are your thoughts on that?" "What other options (or perspectives) are there?" "That's one possibility. What's another?"
  - Acknowledge what was said and then use the union leader technique of asking if there is another point of view—"Who has a different point of view?" Invariably someone will!

Even if a comment is way off track, especially because you are in a group setting, don't reject it outright. At all costs don't embarrass the salesperson with a comment like, "No, that won't work." You will not only offend her but discourage other salespeople from contributing. Even in an open team environment, no one wants to risk "losing face."

Of course you must correct misconceptions and help the group get on the right track, acknowledge, explore, and reshape. For example, "Tim, I am not sure I follow that; can you . . . ?" or "Tim, I see how you might think that. My experience is . . . , and therefore I think it is more effective to. . . . What do others think?" or "Tim, most of the time I think . . . is the best strategy. Perhaps we can discuss that after the meeting."

Round-Robin

To help get a quiet team talking, use the "round-robin" training technique: Ask one salesperson (or recruit a salesperson) to begin, and then go around the room clockwise to get input from each team member. Example: "Great. John, will you begin? Then let's go clockwise around the room to hear from all of you." Round-robin is very effective because usually one person will volunteer, other people know what to expect and have at least a few minutes to prepare, and it gets everyone to contribute.

Role Play

Role playing is very powerful. It is one thing to *talk* about how to do something and another thing to actually *do* it. Rather than just discuss a problem, challenge, or opportunity, ask for volunteers to act it out informally. Assign roles by saying, "Who will be that customer for one minute? Just stay in your own seat. Who wants to deal with this issue as the salesperson for a few minutes?" Ask other salespeople to observe strengths and areas for improvement and take notes so that they can give feedback to the salesperson in the role play. If the role-play volunteer gets stuck, stop the action and coach for a minute or two. By taking a "time out" to discuss what to do and then going back into the role play or swapping roles, you can reduce the pressure on the volunteer in the sales role. Use role playing for development, not as a test.

Keep It Team

Don't allow a team meeting to become a one-on-one discussion. If one salesperson is dominating the discussion, include other perspectives by saying, "Let's hear from some of you who haven't contributed" or, "Let's hear from some people who have not spoken up yet," or suggest continuing the discussion one-on-one after the meeting.

Don't Ignore and Don't Interrupt

It is important not to ignore and not to interrupt. One sales manager was shocked to see how often he did both when he saw a video of himself leading a sales meeting. Not only did he have a habit of interrupting, but when he did on occasion wait until the salesperson was finished speaking, he would totally ignore what the salesperson had said and make his own point, totally unrelated to what the salesperson had said.

> *Use role playing for development, not as a test.*

Unless you respond positively to input by your salespeople, they will quickly clam up, thinking, "Why bother?" The more you listen, the more participation you will get. Most sales managers are surprised to see how much talking they do during a sales meeting and how little their salespeople participate. Sales meetings give you a chance to role-model effective questioning and listening skills: maintain eye contact, acknowledge what was said, ask questions to learn more, drill down, and encourage participation.

Ask for Volunteers

You don't have to call on people to get participation. "Drafting" salespeople puts them on the spot. They may resent it. Moreover, calling on salespeople sets the expectation that it is *you* who will take the initiative. Salespeople who are given a chance to participate voluntarily usually do so willingly and enthusiastically if the environment is one of support.

Ask for volunteers in a way that shows that you *expect* participation. Use your body language (head straight, not tilted; posture straight; confident voice), and wait patiently. If no one volunteers, it's your choice to wait a little longer, ask why no one is participating, encourage, or simply call on a friendly face. Show you *expect* and encourage participation and you will get it.

Clarify Expectations

Set expectations with your sales team about the sales meetings. Encourage active participation. Set standards such as coming on time and review rules for feedback. Clarify how decisions will be made. For example, you may seek team *input* on how to handle leads, but you may be the one to make the final decision. Sales meetings will be motivational when expectations and boundaries are clear.

Network/Politic

If you think that an agenda item is likely to meet with resistance, rather than confronting it alone and cold, think about your team members. Before the sales meeting, approach one (or two) of your key people that you are sure you can count on, prepare that person, and marshal his support.

Sensitivity

Be sensitive in what you say and how you say it. The golden rule for group meetings is, *don't cause anyone to lose face in the presence of others—ever!*

Debrief Every Sales Meeting

The word *debrief* should be the final item on every agenda. At the end of each sales meeting, ask participants for feedback on the strengths and areas for improvement of the meeting. By asking for feedback, you give the team permission to criticize the meeting, themselves, and you.

As salespeople give feedback, listen patiently, take notes, don't be defensive, and thank them for their feedback. Reflect on the feedback and figure out how to use it to improve future sales meetings.

Debriefing also helps salespeople take responsibility for the meeting and assume

> *Sales meetings will be motivational when expectations and boundaries are clear.*

accountability for making meetings better. One coach knew that the process was working when a salesperson said, "I get here on time but have to wait every week for one or two people. If some of us can get here on time, all of us can." True coaching is not a one-coach concept.

Comments such as these are invaluable for making future meetings more productive:

- "Having the specialist come in and talk with us was great. It broke the ice. Now I feel I can call her. We need more of that!"

- "Next time, can we have the material ahead of time so we can prepare?"

■ "Practicing how to ask our customers who else they are talking to was very helpful. In the past I have felt uncomfortable asking questions about the competition."

■ "The cookies were a nice touch. Thanks!"

■ "Can we change rooms? This room is always too hot."

■ "Can we change the time?"

Debriefing helps the group share the responsibility for the successes and failures of the meeting and makes the meetings better.

Interpersonal Factors

As the team becomes more open and more ready for group feedback, the discussions can become more open, too. However, topics that are very specific or personal to one person should always be handled one-on-one.

It is your job to manage the level of dialogue in a meeting. If a salesperson is hostile or rude to a teammate or to you, immediately shut down the communication with a simple comment such as, "Bill, I think it is inappropriate to continue this discussion now. Can we discuss this after the meeting?" or "Let's stick to issues, not make this personal." Move interpersonal issues from the group to behind closed doors.

Logistics of Meetings

Time

At a minimum, set the date for the next sales meeting at the end of the current meeting. Better yet, establish a preset schedule of dates and times based on feedback from the group. Ideally, you can meet with your team weekly, but depending on the situation you might meet monthly or, at a minimum, quarterly. Mix face-to-face and remote meetings in a way that is practical for your team. For remote teams, leverage Webinars and other technology to help keep the meetings interactive. Always let salespeople know the start

> *Move interpersonal issues from the group to behind closed doors.*

and stop times, and keep to the schedule. The approach to meet "until the agenda is covered" is not productive for anyone. Meetings are not marathons. Meetings demand punctuality, and this starts with *you* being on time and expecting the same from your salespeople. Avoid canceling meetings unless circumstances truly warrant it.

One coach says that he cured his group's lateness problem by starting his meeting alone in a room. He said he was already talking when the first person entered the room. Your *behavior*, not your words, will set the standard and tell salespeople how important or unimportant the sales meetings are.

Place

If possible, convene the sales meeting in a place away from phones and other interruptions. A conference room is ideal. It gets you out from behind your desk and sitting *among* team members. As the old Scottish saying goes, "Wherever McTavish sits is the head of the table." Be alert to where your salespeople sit; ask them to fill in so that there are no empty seats between team members, and check that no one is sitting outside of the group. Simply say, "Please join in (move up/in) to help us be more cohesive."

Group Size

Two to three or more people together constitute a meeting. A group of six to eight is ideal, but groups as small as three and as large as 20 or larger can be interactive, too.

Atmosphere

Set a positive atmosphere with refreshments when possible—for example, coffee, tea, juice, and Danish for a 7:30 a.m. meeting or pizza, water, and soft drinks for a 7:00 p.m. meeting.

Sales is a tough job. Salespeople need support. Sales meetings are a way to help the team be a team in spirit, not just structure. Use sales meetings to train, practice, develop, inspire, and showcase. Teams can celebrate successes, dissect failures, plan strategies, evaluate results, and support one another in a way that is not possible one-on-one.

One coach says that he cured his group's lateness problem by starting his meeting alone in a room.

(Please see the Sales Meeting Decision Minutes, Sales Meeting Agenda Planner, and Sales Meeting Checklist at the end of this chapter.)

Sales Meeting Decision Minutes

Decision	Accountability (Who)	Due Date (When)	Result

Sales Meeting Agenda Planner

Sales Manager: _____   Date: _____

Decision Minutes: _____

Agenda

Topics	Objectives	Time	Accountability	Decision	
				Yes	No
				❏	❏
				❏	❏
				❏	❏
				❏	❏
				❏	❏
				❏	❏

Date/Time:

Debriefing/Comments:

Other:

Sales Meeting Checklist

	Yes	No
	❏	❏

Agenda Prepared before the Meeting

	Yes	No
■ Written agenda	❏	❏
■ Sales manager and salespeople contributed to agenda	❏	❏
■ Relevant, high-priority items	❏	❏
■ Topics appropriate for amount of time	❏	❏
■ Salespeople prepared with data and materials prior to meeting as appropriate	❏	❏

Sales Meeting Dynamics and Leadership by Sales Manager

	Yes	No
■ Toured the agenda	❏	❏
■ Guarded the agenda	❏	❏
■ Fostered interactive participation	❏	❏
■ Reached decisions; recorded decision minutes	❏	❏
■ Achieved meeting objectives	❏	❏
■ Debriefed meeting	❏	❏
■ Set date/agenda for next meeting	❏	❏

Time of Meeting, Length, Place

	Yes	No
■ Adequate notice; time convenient to most	❏	❏
■ Started/ended on time	❏	❏
■ Managed time to complete agenda	❏	❏

Meeting Results

	Yes	No
■ Decisions reached	❏	❏
■ Objectives achieved	❏	❏

*S*ales coaching is not a

one-coach concept.

9

Developmental Sales Coaching—Peer and Self-Coaching

Peer Coaching

With a ratio of one sales manager to six to eight or more salespeople, it is important that you identify all resources available to you to help develop your sales team. One Fortune 500 company we work with has a ratio of 28 district managers to more than 2,000 salespeople. Even in organizations where the ratios are manageable, there is too much to do and too much to learn to rely exclusively on sales manager–salesperson development. The flatter the organization, the greater the need to find additional resources of support.

While nothing will replace you as a coach, the process of Developmental Sales Coaching fosters an openness to feedback from others and encourages self-coaching. Just as professional athletes have multiple coaches (for example, for fitness, nutrition, balance, and so on), you can help your salespeople become comfortable with feedback and self-assessment and encourage team members to help one another to reach their goals. Team members are a tremendous resource for feedback because it is often they who have the most information about one another, including the sales manager.

Peer-to-peer coaching is coaching that occurs between two colleagues who view each other as peers and agree to coach each other regardless of what the organization chart says. A good example of the impact of this is a friendship, which, as everyone knows, can be a powerful force for positive change.

Peer coaching is not a coaching session. It is a culture. By fostering feedback among team members, you develop a team that learns to coach itself formally and informally—after calls, in the corridor, on the run—every day.

Because business is global and deliverables are more complex, teams, including virtual teams, have become a way of life in many organizations. Teams must have the ability to manage themselves. A team that is a team *in structure* is very different from a team that is a team *in behavior*. Teams that are teams in structure alone are like a fishnet. Teams that are teams in behavior are like a piece of burlap. Feedback and peer coaching knit the tight weave. When feedback is open and balanced and the intent is to help, the weave is close and the team is close.

Peer coaching is not a coaching session. It is a culture.

Strong teams have lines of communication that are open. Feedback allows them to perform cohesively and to improve continuously. Feedback and peer coaching serve as a glue and help build the relationship among team members needed to achieve their shared objective.

Your behavior in providing consistent coaching, giving balanced feedback, and asking for feedback creates an environment of trust in which peers are more willing to coach one another. However, without feedback and role modeling by you, it's highly unlikely that your salespeople will give or accept feedback from one another.

Certainly it's easier to establish a culture of peer coaching when seniors and other parts of the organization practice it. But even without a culture that supports it, an evaluation or compensation system that rewards it, or the latest technology to make communication easier, your team can be a team. And your success can in some situations influence your organization.

The Peer Coaching/Peer Feedback Challenge

Collaborative learning has become a critical competency in today's sales organization. The ability of salespeople to peer coach and give and accept feedback is essential to maximize the collaborative salesforce tools now available.

Even with your encouragement and example, salespeople at first may be uncomfortable with peer coaching. Tenure, age, ranking, and pay can make salespeople reluctant to give or accept feedback from one another.

While salespeople expect coaching and feedback from you, giving and getting feedback from peers, whether those who are "under" or "over" them, isn't something that many are used to. They see their sales manager as more experienced, knowledgeable, and in an authority position. They see coaching and feedback as the job of the "boss." In some organizations, peer-to-peer coaching can appear to be taboo because levels and titles sharply define who should manage whom. For sales teams to flourish, the tasks and the dynamics between professionals, not titles or structures, must determine who is a peer and how they interact. For peer coaching to work, all team members—in the broadest sense of the term—see one another as peers, whether their rank is higher, lower, or parallel.

Peers who coach one another believe in the value of helping one another to get better. The deal is simple: *"I'll help you be as good as you can be, and you'll help me in the same way."* Mutual trust and commitment and giving balanced feedback prevent the process from becoming competitive, resented, or ignored. The implicit "contract" that salespeople make with one another and with members of the broader team is that they will help one another get better.

Your Role

Because it is outside traditional roles, peer coaching requires encouragement from you. Discuss peer coaching with the members of your team in team meetings and ask them how they feel about looking at their own and each other's performance and honestly and proactively giving feedback to one another. Ask them for their ideas on how peer coaching might work, and seek their commitment. Discuss that, because peers often know more about one another than anyone else, their feedback can be invaluable. Consider formalizing peer coaching, for example, by setting up buddy systems as a part of coaching plans.

Peer coaching is based on the principles of the Developmental Sales Coaching Model. The big difference is that peer coaching is an invitation and requires mutual consent. Compare this example of sales manager coaching versus peer coaching.

- Sales manager to salesperson:

   "Let's meet to debrief your . . . . How's Tuesday?"

- Peer-to-peer (one salesperson to another):

   "How would you feel about meeting on Tuesday to debrief . . . to . . . (benefit) and so we can . . . ?"

Peer Coaching

Peer coaching requires mutual agreement to give and get feedback. It is a two-way street. For example, peer coaching for a team call starts with Peer 1 self-assessing his own strengths and areas for improvement and asking for feedback from Peer 2, and then Peer 2 repeating the process.

For example, "Here's what I think: I thought I handled . . . well . . . by. . . . I am concerned about. . . . What do you see?" Colleague 2 can challenge or question theses statements and provide her feedback. Peer coaching ends with both making a commitment to specific action steps. Or it can be one salesperson going to a peer to say, "Here's how I handled this: . . . . What am I missing? What do you think?"

Salespeople in fact may debrief a team sales call, but they generally focus on the technical aspects of the call (deal, product, customer, follow-up), not their skills, strategy, or teamwork. While a technical debriefing is very important, it is

> *Because it is outside traditional roles, peer coaching requires encouragement from you.*

equally important not to lose the developmental agenda. Without the development piece, the peer coaching won't have as much impact, and participants may become frustrated with the lack of progress. Therefore, it's important to be very clear about the objectives of peer coaching and to stick to them.

Group and Organizational Peer Coaching

Once peer coaching between two colleagues is working, something else can happen. Peer coaching can lead to group peer coaching and organizational coaching. Group-to-group peer coaching is achieved when coaching is extended to the larger group. For example, three or more team members may agree to coach one another. The coaching and feedback usually begin as private (one-on-one) and end up being public (in front of other team members)—unless, of course, the feedback is personal and/or applies only to one colleague.

The benefit of group peer coaching is that everyone can learn from it. For example, when a teammate shouts to a batter who is about to face a wild pitcher, "Lay off the high ones," this helps the other players as well. But since people can feel embarrassed when they get sales manager or peer feedback in a group setting, it is important that the team be ready. If it is offered and accepted in a spirit of trust, feedback helps the salesperson and sales team members improve.

In group peer coaching situations, it is important to avoid becoming a part of a triangle. Encourage team members to represent their own view and take full ownership of what they say. If you or a salesperson do act as "messenger" for a group, you or he must have the permission of the group members to represent them and should clearly articulate that permission and their point of view in the message.

The most far-reaching peer coaching is organizational coaching. It's rare and tremendously powerful when an entire organization embraces feedback and coaching. In this kind of culture, feedback is not viewed as a personal threat. It is taken as an opportunity for improvement. Realistically, this does not mean to suggest that in most organizations, salespeople can give feedback to executives in another division but it does encourage appropriate cross-functional feedback.

> *In group peer coaching situations, it is important to avoid becoming a part of a triangle.*

With the broader definition of peer, coaching can happen coach-to-salesperson, salesperson-to-coach, salesperson-to-salesperson, salesperson-to-colleague, division-to-division, and unit-to-unit. The goal is organization-wide partnering for ongoing improvement. An organization that does this is well positioned for client partnerships.

These questions will help you assess where you and your organization are:

■ Does your organization encourage sales coaching?

■ Do you coach?

- Do most other sales managers coach?

- Where is the majority of coaching time spent—developmental or evaluative? *The more time spent on developmental coaching, the better the performance evaluations and relationship.*

- Who coaches? *Is it just the "bosses" who coach, or is there also peer coaching?*

- What is the quality of the coaching? *Balanced, honest, value-add.*

- Is the predominant environment of the organization one of fear or support? *Fear hampers development. Support fosters it.*

Sales Manager As Peer

You've worked hard to get to where you are—long hours, strong performance, going the extra mile. Without diminishing your role, you can create a peer coaching relationship with your salespeople. Of course you remain the sales manager in the leadership, hierarchical, technical, and administrative sense. But if you are willing to treat your salespeople as peers in the relationship sense—i.e., ask for their perceptions and ideas, learn from their feedback, and not ask of others what you aren't willing to do—you will create an environment in which salespeople are willing to support one another to increase performance.

Almost everyone has had the misfortune of having worked for a "bad" manager. If you Google literature/research on "the bad manager," you will find reams of entries, data, and countless horror stories. But almost nothing is as rewarding as having the experience of working with a "good" manager. And when you ask salespeople or sales managers about the best working relationship they ever experienced with a boss, what they typically describe is more of a collegial relationship than a boss-subordinate one. While the hierarchy said "boss," the relationship felt like peer. In these relationships the people involved experienced trust and professional and personal respect for one another. One of the key differentiators they describe is the open communication that existed.

Far from taking anything from you as a sales manager, creating an environment in which your people are comfortable giving you honest feedback makes your role more fulfilling and your career more rewarding. You will get feedback if you ask for it and your salespeople know that you are open to learning too.

Self-Coaching

You certainly can't be with your salespeople in all of their calls. Often they are out on calls on their own. If they can self-coach, they can learn from every interaction. How you treat their missteps and try to prevent them influences how your salespeople see their own mistakes and how willing they are to self-assess honestly.

For salespeople to want to self-coach, they must be able to get excited (not fearful) about thinking about what they can do better. If you approach their not knowing or accomplishing something as an obstacle, not a failure, they will look at their missteps in the same way. Certainly this is not to say that patterns of failure should not be recognized and dealt with, but the numerous missteps that are bound to happen in sales are opportunities to learn. Salespeople need to see not knowing as one more obstacle to overcome—round one and then round two.

Self-coaching requires each salesperson find the kid within—the excitement of the unknown, the curiosity to ask questions when she doesn't know something and not to be afraid to admit it.

If you ask sales managers and salespeople whose responsibility it is to develop salespeople, most will point to the sales manager. But each salesperson is responsible for his own development. When salespeople self-coach, they take the initiative and assume responsibility for their *own* learning and development.

> *Self-coaching requires each salesperson find the kid within.*

Self-coaching requires stopping the action and creating space, both mentally and physically, to think about performance and answer these three questions:

- What did I do well? Identify and celebrate strengths.

- What are my areas for improvement? Honestly look at ways to be more effective and focus on one priority.

- Where can I go to learn more? Seek an outside view.

The third question is essential. It leads to new information and new perspectives. That additional perspective can come from you or from their peers and customers. For salespeople to ask that question they need an environment where they feel supported and are not afraid to look objectively at their performance and seek feedback.

Self-coaching is a commitment to mastery. One coach was on the right track when he said, "I tell my people that we are busy. I'm here. I'll coach them. But it is also up to them to debrief each call and ask for feedback from me and others and not wait for me or their evaluation to see how they are doing." When salespeople self-coach and seek feedback, they put development in their own hands.

> *Each salesperson is responsible for his own development.*

A wonderful artist and entrepreneur, Ian Woodner, once said that he was his own best model for his paintings. Why? Because the artist and the model got tired at the same time. Similarly, the best coach can be the self-coach—always there when needed to observe, assess, and correct.

*T*he better the coaching,

the higher the score.

10

Performance Reviews and Consequence Coaching

Whether you review performance annually or once a quarter, there are times for you to put on your evaluation cap.

The formal evaluative review usually takes place once a year. It is "game time." Practice is over. Having developed "players" all week, you now choose who will play. Quarterly reviews are often used to supplement annual performance reviews to help red-flag performance problems and to recognize superior performance. The main purpose of the performance review is to evaluate results. But there is also a development component, so there is some attention to the future.

Several factors have turned the performance review into a dreaded event for many salespeople and sales managers alike. Part of this is because, even in organizations in which pay and evaluation are separated, money and job security are attached to the performance review. Another issue is the lack of communication *before* the performance review, which results in salespeople being surprised by the feedback they hear—for the *first* time—causing them to feel that they are being treated unfairly.

But performance reviews don't have to be stressful or cause bad feelings, provided the message delivered is a *summary* of the ongoing feedback and coaching that you have been giving to your salespeople all year.

A performance review is the time to paint a picture of where things stand and what needs to be done going forward. Performance reviews have two objectives:

■ To make sure that salespeople have a clear picture of how they are *perceived* and *rated*—whether the rating is from the sales manager or also includes peers.

■ To begin the developmental process to *improve* the picture for the next performance review.

Evaluative Picture

About 90 percent of the performance review should be dedicated to evaluation so that salespeople have a clear picture of the past. It's your role to provide feedback and a score or ranking to quantify the message. The "score" can be a number, grade, quartile, or scale.

When the scale reflects the big picture, it allows salespeople to understand clearly not only how they are rated, but where they stand relative to others. Salespeople have the right to know how they are perceived. Of course, the stronger their relationship with you and the more consistent your coaching leading up to the review has been,

> *A performance review is the time to paint a picture of where things stand and what needs to be done going forward.*

the more open salespeople will be to the perception. Today technology is making quantifiable information that was once difficult to gather available with one click, and these data help make the rating more objective. In general, the more objective the data, the more successful the performance review. The more consistent the coaching, the more positive the review. When there are no surprises, there are few recriminations.

Development Plan

The remaining 10 percent of the Performance Review time ideally should be dedicated to what salespeople must do to get a better score next time/next year and to begin to create a development plan. Because salespeople may be upset or elated about their ratings, position, money, job security, and so on, it's usually better to introduce the idea of development and set a second meeting the next day or next week (but not as far off as the next month) to begin the development.

The evaluation (grade) makes it clear where the salesperson stands and helps provide the platform for what needs to be developed: The grade is X, and the action plan is Y. The grade is the evaluative piece, and the action plan is the developmental part.

Your Role

Your role in the performance review is to be the messenger—to deliver an *evaluative message* for your *organization* so that your salespeople know where they stand at that point in time. Your message must reflect your ratings and feedback as well as the organization's perception of the salesperson. It can also include peer feedback. Your job is to synthesize the feedback and provide comparative data rel-

ative to others on the team and in the organization so that salespeople have a full picture of where they stand and what they need
to work on to improve and succeed going forward.

You may not be comfortable in performance review situations
in which you have to give a rating if you think the performance
reviews will be fraught with emotion.
For example, one young salesperson was
very upset with her raise. Based on the
feedback she had gotten, she said, "I
thought I was doing great." The manager
replied, "Great for you, but not in com-
parison to others on the team." Clearly
the message surprised her and, because
her manager had never made this perception known, she felt that the evaluation was grossly unfair. Accusations
came both ways and they left the meeting disheartened and upset.

However, by coaching and giving
feedback throughout the year, you can
avoid such counterproductive situations.
Regardless of how hard it is to "paint the
picture," your task is to do this so that
salespeople fully understand how they are rated. While of course you
aim for agreement, it is *not* essential that the salespeople agree with
the evaluation. It is essential, however, that they understand it.

> *Your job is to synthesize the feedback and provide comparative data relative to others on the team and in the organization so that salespeople have a full picture of where they stand and what they need to work on to improve and succeed going forward.*

Preparing for the Performance Review

Use the data that you have to help you organize your feedback and
determine the ratings. Be prepared with balanced feedback and spe-

cific examples to demonstrate that you have done your homework and that you take this responsibility very seriously.

Include in your feedback both quantitative data and impressions—all to paint the picture clearly. It is important to communicate that the review is a *composite* of multiple views, not just yours. The organization's view of how the salespeople rank against one another is a significant part of the review. Sometimes salespeople will object to including things like peer feedback. They may say that they value only your feedback. When this happens, it is essential to support the inclusion of the broader feedback and reinforce the idea that in the organization, other views also count.

To be credible, be prepared to specifically describe any feedback from outside sources. If you have any questions about a part of the picture that a peer paints, you must go to the source and ask what it means. When one sales manager was told that one of her salespeople wasn't "crisp," she approached the specialist who had provided the feedback to learn more about his observation and get specific behavioral examples.

Another sales manager questioned a third-quartile ranking that a team member gave to a peer so that she could understand it and represent the peer's perspective accurately.

Once you have gathered your data and prepared your balanced feedback, work out the score.

Your preparation is only half of the job. Preparation is also the responsibility of your salespeople. Give them ample time to prepare so that they are ready to discuss their performance and give their view of their rating. If at all possible, allow one week prior to the performance review so that they may prepare.

You can facilitate salespeople's preparation by giving them a self-evaluation form to complete. But remember that a performance review is a dialogue, *not* a form. Encourage salespeople to really think about their performance in depth. Ideally, the form you give them will make it easier for them to self-assess during the meeting. Often, they are harder on themselves than you will be. Their impression is just that, and unless the circumstances are extreme and significant new information is revealed, do *not* accept excuses or change your score.

Performance reviews can be emotional. If you have feelings of discomfort about performance reviews, it is important that you confront those feelings and attitudes so that your own hesitations aren't communicated to your salespeople and to make sure that you are able to provide a clear and helpful message.

By managing logistics, you can help create the best atmosphere. Whenever possible, select a neutral setting other than your office (for example, a small conference room) and sit next to the salesperson to create a collegial setting. You don't need the status of sitting behind your desk in your office to reinforce your authority. If your office is your only option, when possible sit at a table rather than behind your desk.

Schedule sufficient time to have a full discussion. In general, about 30 to 45 minutes is adequate. Treat the time as sacred. One sales manager sent the wrong signals when he *started* the meeting by saying, "We have *only* one-half hour," and then took phone calls during that time.

Most organizations conduct performance reviews annually. Ideally these are supplemented by quarterly reviews, which, in turn, are supported by Developmental Sales Coaching.

The Performance Review Model

The Performance Review Model is divided into two parts. The first, the evaluative part, makes up 90 percent of the meeting. The second is the developmental part. Development is optional, based on whether or not the salesperson chooses to begin to plan for the coming period or year.

The Evaluative Segment

The evaluative segment of the Performance Review is made up of three parts: Connect and Purpose, Perceptions, and Rating.

Connect and Purpose

Because performance reviews can be stressful, to help ease into the discussion, begin with *rapport*. Rapport can be brief. The key is to make it genuine. Once you've built rapport to help the salesperson feel more comfortable, describe the *dual purpose* of the meeting: (1) to review performance and (2) to discuss plans for the next year.

For example, "Terri, we have two objectives. First, I'm going to ask for your perceptions and then present my evaluation and that of the organization. It is a 'snapshot' of the last year, and I hope you find that it's a pretty good likeness—both of your strengths and of your areas for improvement. Then we will talk about next year and how to make it better. This is very important. We can talk about development today, or we can set a meeting to begin development in the next week."

Connecting and purpose set the stage. They set the focus and show that you are there to support the salesperson. Do *not* open with the number or grade. One sales manager started fireworks when he began by saying, "You're a three."

Perceptions

Ask salespeople for their perceptions of their performance and then ask for their self-rating. The "they talk first" process gives salespeople an opportunity to present their perspective. One sales manager who was hesitant to do this was amazed at how much it helped. In advance of the performance review, he asked a salesperson to think about his performance for the year and asked him to consider several things:

> *Ask salespeople for their perceptions of their performance and then ask for their self-rating.*

- What did he do well? (During the meeting, the sales manager had to push the salesperson to discuss his strengths. He wanted to focus on the negatives.)
- What did he think were his areas for improvement?
- How well did he achieve his objectives?
- What did he think his rating should be, and why?
- What are areas to focus on for development for the coming year?

Even though in this situation the sales manager disagreed with much of what the salesperson said, by hearing his perspective, the sales manager was able to paint the picture more clearly because she saw what she had to adjust in *the salesperson's* picture. The sales manager used examples to paint a compelling picture, which the salesperson accepted. And the salesperson was more open to the sales manager's feedback because he felt that his view had been heard.

After the salesperson has described/painted a picture of his strengths and areas for improvement, provide your specific feedback on his strengths and areas for improvement and support it with examples and/or metrics.

Rating

Before you give your rating, give the salesperson the opportunity to share with you her view of what the rating should be. Probe as necessary, then provide your rating and support it. When the grade or rating suggested by the salesperson is aligned with your rating, you'll probably move the session into the developmental segment more quickly.

If there is not agreement, don't change your grade. While there may be circumstances that can cause you to change your rating, these situations should be very rare—2 percent of the time. You would have to be very, very far off before you adjust your picture because it was not accurate. Don't change your review if you are off by only 5 percent. Differences are almost inevitable, and disappointments despite coaching are also common. With ongoing feedback, preparation, and analysis of the data, you can be fair and accurate.

To ensure that there is a clear understanding, ask the salesperson to summarize the review and what he got out of the discussion. The salesperson may not agree with it (ideally he will), but he must understand it.

Option to Move into the Developmental Segment

Ask the salesperson if she would like to move into the development phase to discuss how to make the next year better. If the answer is no, agree on the next steps and set a date for the development/performance plan meeting. The purpose of this meeting is to determine development objectives for the coming year or quarter and ideally begin to develop the coaching plan for the coming year. (Please see the discussion of coaching plans in Chapter 6.)

To know whether to proceed to the developmental segment, simply ask, "Are you up for the developmental discussion to help make next year's picture better?" If the salesperson opts to begin discussing development, start the process with a comment such as, "Let's take a look at what we need to accomplish next year" to help the salesperson think about what he should focus on for the coming year, and then give your view.

Discuss what to focus on to make the next year better, and then set a time to finalize the coaching plan for the coming quarter or year. In all likelihood, developing the coaching plan will run into the next meeting, after both the salesperson and you have had a chance to think about it. The coaching plan is the template and criteria for the coaching and performance evaluation for each quarter (or whatever period of time you agree to). The best advice for developing a coaching plan is to create clear, measurable objectives for each quarter and to keep the plan clear and simple.

To end the performance review, discuss what you and the organization can do to support the salesperson. Wrap up the session with a thank-you and encouragement. This development part of the meeting should make up no more than 10 percent of performance review time.

When a performance review has not been positive, it's usually better to postpone beginning the development plan meeting because the salesperson may be too preoccupied to focus on the next steps. Even when the session has been very positive, the salesperson may be too exhilarated about the positives to think about ways to improve.

Guidelines for Leading the Performance Review

In summary:

- Allow time for you and the salesperson to prepare.

- Be frank. Don't hedge.

- *Set the dual purpose as you connect.*

- Ask questions. Don't do all the talking.

- If the meeting is going badly, i.e., if emotions are running high, acknowledge it and discuss it. If you can't turn it around, offer to reschedule.

- Begin with the positives. Don't start with the hardest point first.

- Don't start with a grade or score.

- Don't let the meeting be a big bang. Provide Developmental Sales Coaching all year to avoid trauma and shock!

- Set a positive tone from the outset.

- Once you give a score, set a plan to make things better for the next review.

- Don't change your grade.

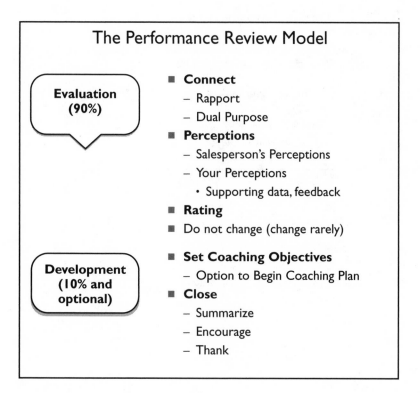

The Performance Review Model

Evaluation (90%)

- **Connect**
  - Rapport
  - Dual Purpose
- **Perceptions**
  - Salesperson's Perceptions
  - Your Perceptions
    - Supporting data, feedback
- **Rating**
- Do not change (change rarely)

Development (10% and optional)

- **Set Coaching Objectives**
  - Option to Begin Coaching Plan
- **Close**
  - Summarize
  - Encourage
  - Thank

Self-Critique after the Performance Review

After each performance review, take a moment to self-critique.
Use this checklist:

	Yes	No
■ Paved the way for the performance review with ongoing Developmental Sales Coaching.	❑	❑
■ Prepared and gave the salesperson the opportunity to prepare.	❑	❑
■ Demonstrated a positive attitude.	❑	❑
■ Set the dual purpose.	❑	❑
■ Elicited the salesperson's perception.	❑	❑
■ Provided self and organizational feedback and rating.	❑	❑
■ Began or set plans for developmental meeting.	❑	❑
■ Encouraged the salesperson.	❑	❑
■ Did not change grade (unless major new information became available)	❑	❑

Annual Relationship Review

Just as you lead performance reviews, it is very helpful to lead a relationship review with each salesperson. The agenda for this meeting, which should be scheduled with every salesperson once a year, focuses solely on the state of the relationship between the salesperson and you. In this meeting you ask:

- "What am I doing that's getting in your way?" or "What should I be doing less of?"

- "What can I do to be more helpful?" or "What am I doing that I should be doing more of?"

- "What do we need to do differently (that we can control) to make our relationship stronger?"

Consequence Coaching

As all sales coaches know, there are times when regardless of the amount of support they give, some salespeople won't make the grade. Once you've exhausted all avenues of development, as a last effort to turn the situation around, switch your mode of coaching from developmental to consequence. The *Consequence Coaching* Model addresses *performance problems* that have been *ongoing*.

Consequence Coaching is based on Developmental Sales Coaching with one very big difference: instead of "asking," you tell. In many organizations, it is the coaching that is provided in an intense 90-day coaching cycle during the probationary period.

Because you have seen little or no progress from previous coaching sessions and often a half-hearted effort, you probably have already given informal warnings. The two big challenges with Consequence Coaching are:

- Delivering the message in a very clear way

■ Differentiating real obstacles (a truly new circumstance that has legitimately impeded progress) from excuses so that you are not swayed by excuses

As the name suggests, the objective of Consequence Coaching is to spell out in no uncertain terms the standards that the salesperson must meet and what she will face if she fails to meet these standards. The words "they talk first" are not the driving force in Consequence Coaching. Consequence Coaching makes the shift to evaluation. At this point, you are no longer asking the salesperson for her perception because you have already done that several times over.

Consequence Coaching is developmental in that the goal is to provide support to help the salesperson *improve* and succeed. It is evaluative in that it provides hard measurements and sets standards and consequences if the metrics are not met.

Begin by summarizing the previous agreement or objectives and ask whether or not the salesperson has met them. If the objectives have not been met and/or there has been little progress, it is very important, unless there are new, significant circumstances (not excuses), that you do *not* change your message. Do not ask the salesperson for his perceptions or why, since you have already been down that path several times. State your perception of where things stand based on the data you have, describe what is unacceptable about the situation, define the specific measurable standards that the salesperson must meet and the time frame for meeting them, and state the *consequences* of not meeting them.

The salesperson may not agree with the message, but it's your role to make sure that she clearly understands it and the consequences. Depending on the situation, the salesperson can be placed informally or formally on notice. Before this meeting, you may wish to seek guidance from your Human Resources group.

The Consequence Coaching Model is made up of five steps.

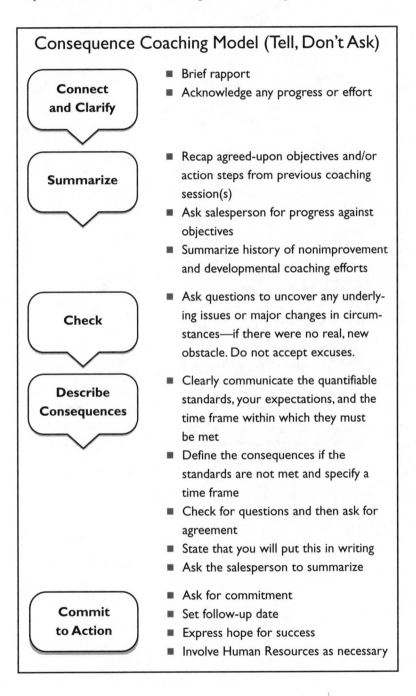

Consequence Coaching Model (Tell, Don't Ask)

Connect and Clarify
- Brief rapport
- Acknowledge any progress or effort

Summarize
- Recap agreed-upon objectives and/or action steps from previous coaching session(s)
- Ask salesperson for progress against objectives
- Summarize history of nonimprovement and developmental coaching efforts

Check
- Ask questions to uncover any underlying issues or major changes in circumstances—if there were no real, new obstacle. Do not accept excuses.

Describe Consequences
- Clearly communicate the quantifiable standards, your expectations, and the time frame within which they must be met
- Define the consequences if the standards are not met and specify a time frame
- Check for questions and then ask for agreement
- State that you will put this in writing
- Ask the salesperson to summarize

Commit to Action
- Ask for commitment
- Set follow-up date
- Express hope for success
- Involve Human Resources as necessary

R2-D2, you know better

than to trust a strange computer.

C-3PO, Star Wars

11

Developmental Sales Coaching—Technology As a Sales Coaching Tool

A book on sales coaching wouldn't be complete today without addressing the technology available to sales managers to help them increase the productivity of their salespeople and achieve revenue growth. Organizations are keenly aware of the role of sales coaching in increasing sales-force productivity. They recognize that by focusing on the area of sales, they can achieve revenue growth. While they continue to look at people and processes, technology is now the third critical element for achieving that growth.

Finding the right technology and identifying practical ways to leverage the data from the technology is the new frontier of sales management. Many organizations have installed sales force automation (SFA) and/or customer relationship management (CRM) programs to capture and leverage data. Information that once was time-consuming and laborious to gather or was simply not available is now a click away.

One of the problems with SFA and CRM is that for years companies have struggled with user adoption. In many organizations, this continues to be an issue. Salespeople will resist using any system if they believe it exists just to keep tabs on them and evaluate them rather than to help them.

Many years ago, I was a teacher and principal in the Philadelphia and New York City school systems. I found that when students complained about a class, much more often than not, their concerns were justified. This observation carried over to my life in corporate education. When salespeople complained about their training, more often than not the complaints were valid—the programs were irrelevant, not customized to their needs or their business, not interactive, lacked follow-up, and so on. Unfortunately, it seems the same dynamic exists with how salespeople feel about some SFA and CRM systems. First and foremost, salespeople will vehemently

> *Salespeople will resist using any system if they believe it exists just to keep tabs on them and evaluate them rather than to help them.*

resist using these systems if they don't feel that they are deriving any benefit or if they see the systems as tools for managers to micromanage or punish them. When they view a system as an evaluation tool rather than a support tool, they won't be motivated to use it. When, on top of that, the system is cumbersome, slow, and complex, and populating it is frustrating, resistance only increases. One of the first steps in making technology work is to objectively assess the system you have in place and do everything that is possible and practical to provide your salespeople with a tool that is valuable to them and is friendly to salespeople and you (i.e., fast).

Getting salespeople to use a system that works for *them* is doable. If you think about the Internet, today there are more than one billion users. Few of them have ever taken a course. Few of them have been forced into using it. They use the Internet because it is easy to use, provides value to them, and meets their needs. The challenge of user adoption with SFAs and CRMs can be met in two ways:

■ Provide salespeople with the right technology so that they view it as a tool to help them succeed—one sales manager said, "The key is to do the technology right."

■ Be relentless in role modeling and reinforcing the use of the technology every day.

The question is, how do you "do it right"? You start by selecting a system that meets the needs of the sales force. Research with experts, sales managers, and salespeople has identified these criteria for selecting a system:

■ Easy to use at the salesperson and sales manager level

■ High adoption rates (rates can vary from 25 to 95 percent)

■ High speed to deployment (up and running and valuable to at least one division within a few months rather than 1 year or more)

■ Tools that are of practical use to sales managers and salespeople

■ Total cost of ownership (ROI including cost of managing and updating)

But the most important aspect of a sales automation system is that it is driven by the needs of salespeople and sales managers. The objective should be to help salespeople be more productive.

Because salespeople have a tendency to look at the SFA and CRM as "big brother," changing that perception takes training so the sales force understands why and how to populate any system. They also need role modeling to reinforce the many compelling benefits to them. The more salespeople experience the benefits to them, the faster and better the systems will work for them and for you.

Benefits to the Sales Force

Adoption by your salespeople begins with you. Salespeople will use the technology if they believe that you are seriously committed to it as a part of the sales process. One of the most important benefits of SFA is the *discipline* it imposes on salespeople to *analyze their sales activity* and continue to make *judgments* and *decisions* and to give them the resources and support they need to win business.

> *Adoption by your salespeople begins with you. Salespeople will use the technology if they believe that you are seriously committed to it as a part of the sales process.*

Entering data encourages salespeople to continue to analyze, make judgment calls, and plan strategies as well as to tap into and get access to the resources they need if they are to win.

Other important benefits of technology include:

- Gaining easy access to information so that they can be more responsive to their customers.

- Collaborating with team members who are involved in supporting their deal or keeping team members posted who work with the customer even if they are not involved in this specific deal.

- Maximizing their time by reducing preparation time, thereby increasing sales time.

- Providing fast access to best practices, refreshers, case studies, RFP data, competitive information, and so on.

- Eliminating unnecessary dialogues with sales managers about mundane information. For example, sales managers can go to the SFA for data about what is in the pipeline so that time can be spent planning strategies, developing skills, and winning deals.

- Learning and connecting with customers and maximizing use of networking tools.

- Managing and tracking their pipeline to accelerate closing.

- Speeding the sales process with tools such as Webinars.

- Getting on an equal playing field with customers who now have so much information on them and their competitors.

All the information that was previously passed down (and sometimes lost) by word of mouth is there with one click—*if*, of course, high-quality and timely data are entered and the system is used.

Benefits to You

Technology can give you full visibility into the sales cycle so you can have access to metrics to follow and support opportunities from the pipeline stage through closing and postclosing. For example, you can be alerted, sometimes in real time, to where deals stand and where resources and coaching are needed. So if you see that a deal is stalled at a particular phase of the sales process, such as getting to the economic decision maker, you can coach the salesperson and share ideas on how to uptier, or a team member can leverage a colleague who has a relationship with the decision maker. One sales manager relies on her dashboard to know where important deals are, what products are being sold, and where salespeople rank in the territory to pinpoint areas for support and coaching. Another sales manager uses his "deal alerts," which generate e-mails to seniors and sales managers to let them know about a deal that is in danger of being lost so that they can put resources on it. Notices can also be sent out for deals won so that success can be recognized.

Sales 2.0 tools can provide:

- Immediate access to information such as knowing what is going on with salespeople.

- A dashboard, a data interface that presents high-level information that you can easily drill into to monitor and coach to your salespeople's needs—for example, determining the number of RFPs generated and close ratios, identifying bottlenecks, and becoming aware of changes such as longer sales cycles.

- Immediate access to data on the pipeline and status against metrics.

- Visibility—for example, if a big deal hits the dashboard.

- More time to coach on strategies on how to win rather than getting information that is available from the system, such as top opportunities.

- Notification of problems so that you can give the support needed. One sales manager who is a strong proponent of his company's SFA tells his salespeople, "No one will be fired for losing a deal. But there is a real problem if you haven't entered data into our app (application) to alert us so that we can put resources on it." While of course he doesn't want to lose a deal, his approach is that a loss is palatable *if* the sales force has done all it could to win the business.

- Real-time data to celebrate success and debrief lost deals. As one sales manager said: "It's really bad to lose. It's worse to lose and not get intelligence. We must learn from our losses."

- A way to motivate by sharing data on wins and sales-force rankings.

- Objective performance data to support your observations and perceptions and direct your coaching.

Technology can help you reduce dependency on classroom training and help put training in the hands of sales managers and salespeople. There are so many changes in markets, products, and competitors, but there is a limit to how much training can and should be delivered in the classroom. Alternatives in the form of e-learning, Webinars, VODs, just-in-time performance support tools, or podcasts won't replace the classroom, but they provide a power-ful complement and supplement to classroom training.

The challenges for you are to find practical ways to use the data to coach and manage, using the technology not only as a strategy planning and evaluation tool, but to help salespeople manage their sales efforts, improve their sales performance, and empower them with fast access to information about their customers and prospects. You can *turn the input entered by salespeople into output that you use to lead your team.*

One organization did just that. It created a dashboard in which it identified performance metrics for sales productivity, including number of calls per day, number of customers contacted over a 90-day period by a salesperson, customer retention rate, new business, and cross-selling. Under each metric, it defined several behaviors to provide a quantitative and qualitative dimension. It also provided sales managers with coaching questions to support each metric. The company then compiled the data submitted by salespeople across geographies and regions down to the individual sales manager and salesperson level and used these data to dramat-

> *You can* turn the input entered by salespeople into output that you use to lead your team.

ically improve performance. Sales managers used the data to specifically focus their coaching—whom to coach and what to coach. For example, if a region had a low closing ratio, they provided closing training modules. If the problem were limited to a few salespeople, that became the focus of individual coaching. When they realized that the number of calls per day was a big issue globally, they placed an intense focus on calls per day.

The results for the company's sales force of 2,000 salespeople were staggering in the impact on improved productivity:

■ 462,000 additional sales calls were made each year by face-to-face sales force.

■ 967,000 additional calls were made each year by the call center salespeople.

This activity resulted in a 21 percent improvement in sales and generated $747 million in *additional* revenue.

Another organization used data from its application to help set standards for performance. Metrics from country to country revealed that there were major differences in the amount of face time salespeople spent "in the moment" with their customers. Accounting for country differences such as the economy and the travel time, they saw a clear correlation between face time and productivity. The lowest-performing country reported that 16 percent of salespeople's time was spent with customers. The highest-performing country had 27 percent of the salespeople's time spent with customers. By drawing attention to the differences, the company set a standard that face-to-face time was not to go below 25 percent, and it is working toward 40 to 50 percent. It took steps to remove some of the administrative tasks from salespeople, automate some other systems, and provide one administrative assistant for every five salespeople in certain regions. Of course, the specifics will change based on the business, but the use of the data is compelling and the application across businesses is clear.

What can you do if your organization doesn't provide you with the technology and the data aren't available to support you and your sales team? Let your management, head of sales, and head of IT know that you are *not* getting the information you need. Describe what you need from a system, how you will use it, and the impact it could have on performance. Do research on the Web to learn about Internet-based tools or the more traditional client/server applications. Find a senior manager to champion the initiative. Talk to other sales managers. Suggest bringing in providers to talk with you, other managers, and senior management. Get a demo. Ask for a pilot. Be the champion yourself. Remember, the technology is not the point. It is a practical application to help your sales team improve. It's all about the practical tools, not the technology.

Today, sales coaching truly has a third dimension.

The first two dimensions are:

- People (hiring, leading, training, reinforcing, measuring, rewarding)

- Processes (procedures that provide the foundation)

Technology is the third dimension. It is electronic word of mouth allowing for real-time information, collaboration, and training. Data from technology can be used to develop strategies, set the focus of sales coaching, and individualize training to the needs of salespeople. Technology can be your virtual sales support system—always one click away.

We each have an inner coach.

The sales manager's job is to

give that coach a voice.

Conclusion

More than 25 years ago, when I was a principal of a New York City high school, nothing told more about what was going on in a school than its corridors. Based on my experience in working with hundreds of organizations globally, I believe that the key indicator of the culture of a sales organization is the level of sales coaching that happens more formally and "in the halls" every day. The culture of a sales organization is what its sales managers do every day.

The Developmental Sales Coaching approach described in this book is more than a model and a set of techniques. It is a way of life for you, your team, and your organization. Once ongoing coaching and feedback are a part of the DNA of how you manage, you and your sales team will be hard to beat.

Today effective sales coaching is more achievable than ever before. Organizations are ready for it. The technology is there to support it. Your sales team needs it. And you are there to provide it.

Through Developmental Sales Coaching, you send a message: "We are good now. We can be even better." It is truly a leap for everyone—a commitment to working to get to the next level and the level beyond that.

Sales is an area that, when focused on, can be dramatically improved. No one in a sales organization is in a better position to achieve that dramatic improvement than you. You can teach your salespeople to analyze situations, develop practical and creative solutions, and achieve results. Your coaching efforts will lead to increased revenue and stronger customer and internal relationships. To make coaching a way of life for you and your team, each day ask yourself: What did we do well? What can we do better? Where can we go to learn more?

Every sales manager has a coach within. By giving your coach a voice, you will help your salespeople, your organization, and you achieve your goals.

Appendix

Coaching Tools

The following worksheets will support sales managers in their coaching efforts:

Index

About the Author

Linda Richardson is the founder and executive chairwoman of Richardson, a global sales training and consulting firm. A recognized leader in the sales training and sales management world, Linda has won the coveted Stevie Award for Lifetime Achievement in Sales Excellence and was identified in 2007 by Training Industry Inc. as one of the "Top 20 Most Influential Training Professionals." Linda has authored 10 books on selling and sales management, including her most recent *New York Times* best seller, *Perfect Selling*, and her series of 15-minute audio books, NanoSalesBooks.

Linda also teaches sales at Wharton Graduate School of the University of Pennsylvania and Wharton Executive Development Center. Her clients include Goldman Sachs, Cisco, Google, Vanguard, KPMG, PricewaterhouseCoopers, Pfizer, and Shell.

Additional information on Richardson is available at www.richardson.com or (215) 940-9255.